GOD AT 2000

Edited by
Marcus Borg and Ross Mackenzie

MOREHOUSE PUBLISHING
HARRISBURG, PENNSYLVANIA

Morehouse Publishing
P.O. Box 1321
Harrisburg, PA 17105

Morehouse Publishing is a Continuum imprint.

Chapter 3 of this book, "An Ocean of God: The Interconnectedness of All Being," © 2000 by Lawrence Kushner. "Virtual Reality" and "Stranger on the Bus" excerpted from *Invisible Lives of Connection: Sacred Stories of the Ordinary* © 1996 by Lawrence Kushner (Woodstock, Vt.: Jewish Lights Publishing). Permission granted by Jewish Lights Publishing, Woodstock, Vt.

Cover design by Corey Kent.

Borg, Marcus.
    God at 2000 / Marcus Borg and Ross Mackenzie.
        p.   cm
    ISBN 0-8192-1907-X (alk. paper)
    1. God. 2. Faith. I. Title: God at two thousand. II. Mackenzie, Ross, 1927-III. Title.

    BT012 .B557 2000
    231—dc21
                                                          00-061682

Printed in the United States of America

02 03 04 05   10 9 8 7 6 5 4 3

GOD AT 2000

Contents

Introduction

This book is the result of "God at 2000," a nationally televised symposium that took place at Oregon State University in February 2000. The event was jointly sponsored by the Hundere Endowment for Religion and Culture at Oregon State; the Chautauqua Institution of Chautauqua, New York; and Trinity Institute of Trinity Parish, New York City.

"God at 2000" featured seven well-known religious thinkers and authors from the three major Western religions. In alphabetical order, the lecturers were Karen Armstrong, Marcus Borg, Joan Chittister, Diana Eck, Lawrence Kushner, Seyyed Hossein Nasr, and Desmond Tutu. They are introduced more fully later in this book at the beginning of the chapters containing their lectures.

A sellout audience of almost 1,200 people attended "God at 2000" in person at Oregon State in Corvallis, Oregon. Thousands more watched it live at satellite television downlink sites around the country. It was also Webcast live on the Internet, both audio and video, and thus reached many people in their homes in North America and overseas. Participants at off-site locations took part in the question-and-response sessions by telephone, fax, and e-mail. It was an exciting and highly successful event.

The chapters in this book are not an exact transcript of what was said at "God at 2000." The speakers had the opportunity to revise their talks for publication. The book also includes the question-and-response session that followed each lecture, a chapter reporting the panel discussion at the end of the event, and a concluding epilogue in which we, as the editors of this volume, share some impressions.

The content of the lectures in this book is suggested by the assignment given to the speakers. They were invited to address the personal question "How I See God," or "How I see 'the sacred.'" All of them have spent most of their lives studying, thinking, writing, and talking about God, as well as wrestling with God. And so the question presented to them was "From your lifetime of study, reflection, and experience, what have you learned about God that seems most important to you?" We asked them to be personal, and in their different ways, they were.

"God at 2000" had two premises. The first is that how we think about God matters. Our ideas about God—our concepts and images of the sacred—shape our sense of the reality or unreality of God, our sense of God's character, and our perception of what life with God is about.

The second is that how we think and talk about God changes over time. We refer not simply to how our ideas about God change in the course of our individual journeys from childhood through adolescence and into the stages of adulthood, but also to cultural developments that change how God is thought of and spoken about. How people thought about God in the year 1000 was significantly different from how people think about God in the year 2000.

To speak of a shorter unit of time, how we think and talk about God at the beginning of the 21st century is different in important ways from how people did a hundred years ago because of developments in the last century. These developments include our growing awareness of religious pluralism, the feminist critique of the patriarchal character of much of traditional religion, the emergence of liberation theologies, a greater awareness of the relationship between God and the natural world, and changes in the religion and science debate generated by postmodern science.

Some people believe that God is the same yesterday, today, and tomorrow. They could be right, though what is known as "process theology" would disagree. But whether or not God changes, how we as humans think about God does change. "God at 2000" seeks to describe, among other things, the changing ways in which we think and talk about God at the beginning of the 21st century.

There are many people to thank for the role they played in making "God at 2000" successful. Above all, special gratitude is due to Al Hundere, a 1938 engineering graduate from Oregon State University who lived much of his adult life in San Antonio, Texas. Al Hundere made a major gift to Oregon State just over six years ago that created the Hundere Endowment and Chair of Religion and Culture in the Philosophy Department. Al is no longer with us, at least not on this plane of existence: He died in October 1996. But his generosity has created a lasting legacy, and has made much possible, including "Jesus at 2000" at Oregon State four years ago, and now "God at 2000."

We also want to thank a number of individuals from the sponsoring institutions.

From Chautauqua: President Daniel L. Bratton, Thomas L. Becker, and Judy Bloomquist not only attended the event in person, but provided much support in the months before to the Reverend Dr. Ross Mackenzie, the person primarily responsible for Chautauqua's participation and one of the coeditors of this book.

From Trinity Institute and the Episcopal Cathedral Teleconferencing Network (ECTN): The Reverend Dr. Frederic B. Burnham, the Reverend Dr. Daniel Matthews, and Linda Hannick.

From Oregon State University: Dr. Judy Ringle, assistant to Marcus Borg, was the primary administrator of the event and accomplished a Herculean task with remarkable efficiency, competence, and good spirits. A very able team of student workers assisted her: Basye Holland-Shuey, Erica Porter, Leah Hall, Tom Eckart, and B. Patrick Williams; and Lois Summers and Sandra Davis, office staff in the Philosophy Department. All of them were remarkable, and we are very grateful to them for the immense amount of work they did.

1 Seeing God Again: What's at Stake
Marcus Borg

Marcus Borg is Hundere Distinguished Professor of Religion and Culture in the Philosophy Department at Oregon State University. Internationally known in both academic and church circles as a scholar and lecturer, he is the author of ten books, including the best-selling *Meeting Jesus Again for the First Time* and *The God We Never Knew*, named by *Publishers Weekly* as one of the ten best books in religion for 1997. His most recent book is *The Meaning of Jesus: Two Visions*, a dialogue with N.T. Wright, a well-known British scholar. It won the award for "Best General Interest Book of 1999" from the Association of Theological Booksellers.

Other books include: *Conflict, Holiness and Politics in the Teaching of Jesus; Jesus: A New Vision; Jesus in Contemporary Scholarship;* and *Jesus at 2000*.

In addition, he is the coeditor of two books: *The Lost Gospel Q* and *Jesus and Buddha: The Parallel Sayings*.

Described by *The New York Times* as "a leading figure among the new generation of Jesus scholars," Borg is a Fellow of the Jesus Seminar and has been national chair of the Historical Jesus Section of the Society of Biblical Literature and cochair of its International New Testament Program Committee. He has appeared on NBC's *Today Show*, PBS's *Newshour*, NPR's *Fresh Air*, and ABC's Peter Jennings *Primetime*. His books have been translated into seven languages, and he has lectured widely to both academic and church audiences throughout North America and overseas (England, Scotland, Austria, Germany, Belgium, Hungary, Israel, Scotland, and South Africa).

Borg earned his bachelor's degree from Concordia College (Minnesota), and his master's and doctor's degrees from Oxford University. Before coming to OSU in 1979, Borg held teaching positions at Carleton College, South Dakota State University, and Concordia

College. He has been a visiting professor at the University of Puget Sound and Pacific School of Religion in Berkeley.

As a professor here at Oregon State University and thus the "local boy" among your speakers, I want to welcome you on behalf of the university to "God at 2000." We are very pleased that you are here, and pleased to have so many people elsewhere participating in this event that comes to you from a small town in Oregon.

The title of my lecture is "Seeing God Again: What's at Stake." When I sent out letters of invitation to our speakers, I invited them to be personal as they addressed the question, "How I see God/the sacred."

I decided to follow my own directions quite literally: From the whole course of my life thus far I will talk about what I have learned about God that seems most important to me. Thus, when I turn to the body of my talk, I will organize it around six statements, each beginning with the sentence stem, "I have learned that . . ."

As I do so, I speak as a Christian. I grew up as a Lutheran, and am now an Episcopalian. Moreover, I am a nonliteralistic and nonexclusivist kind of Christian. What I mean by these words will, I trust, become clear in my lecture.

As a Christian, I will focus primarily on ways of seeing God within the Christian tradition. I do so for two reasons. On the one hand, the Christian tradition is what I know best. On the other hand, I am convinced that one of the most important issues in the church today is the question of God—the question of "how we see God."

When I speak about seeing God, I mean in a comprehensive sense how we think about God, including both our concepts and images of God. Our concepts of God shape how we imagine God and God's relationship to the universe. Our images of God shape how we see God's character.

How we see God matters. It matters not because God wants us to get it right, as if what God is most concerned about is correct ideas and beliefs. Rather, it matters because how we see God matters to us. Our concepts of God can make God seem real or unreal, remote or near. Our images of God shape our sense of the character of God and of what taking God seriously is about, indeed what the Christian life is about.

The title of my lecture speaks not only of seeing God, but also of seeing God again. The premise of this part of my title is the realization that ideas about God change over time. Though God may (or may not be) the same yesterday, today, and tomorrow, our ideas about God do change. They have a history, as Karen Armstrong has so impressively shown in her book, A History of God. [1]

I am convinced that we live in a time in the life of our culture and the church when an older set of ideas about God needs to change. An older and very common way of seeing God has become problematic for millions of people in our time. These millions include many Christians, as well as many who were raised in the church but then left, becoming part of what Episcopal Bishop John Spong has called "the church alumni association."

This older conventional Christian way of seeing God was serviceable for centuries. It worked for millions of Christians for a very long time. But in our time, for many, this older way of seeing God has made the notion of God incredible or doubtful. For many others, who continue to believe in God, or at least try to, it has made the notion of God dysfunctional in their lives, causing more grief than good. Thus I am convinced that a major need in the church in North America today is "seeing God again."

What I Have Learned about God

This older conventional way of seeing God is what I grew up with. And so, as I now move to the main body of my talk—six statements crystallizing "what I have learned about God that seems most important to me"—I will use the pattern, "How I saw God the first time," and "Seeing God again—how I see God now."

God is known in all of the enduring religious traditions of the world

I have learned that God is known in all of the enduring religious traditions of the world. My first affirmation is not simply modern or postmodern political correctness or liberal tolerance. Rather, I have been persuaded of its truth by the study of other religions and from personal acquaintance with people of other religions.

It is very different from how I saw God the first time. I grew up in a time and place where it was taken for granted that Christianity was the only true religion and Jesus the only way of salvation. That is why we had missionaries: It was crucial that nonChristians hear about Christianity.

It now seems clear to me that God is known across cultures in all of the enduring religions. I find it literally incredible to think that the God of the whole universe has chosen to be known in only one religious tradition, which just fortunately happens to be our own. Indeed, if I thought that being a Christian meant believing that Christianity is the only true religion, I could not be one.

Common as this exclusivist claim has been in Christian history, I do not think it is intrinsic to Christianity. Moreover, I do not think it diminishes Christianity at all to see it as one of the world's great religions, and not as the only true religion. It is the other way around: When Christians claim that Christianity is the only true religion, its credibility suffers greatly. But when Christianity is seen as one of the world's great religions, it gains enormous credibility.

A major task for Christians in the twenty-first century is grateful and enthusiastic affirmation of religious pluralism. This means accepting a relative status for Christianity, but a relative status as one of the magnificent first-magnitude stars in the constellation of the world's religions.

God or the sacred is ineffable

I have learned that God or the sacred is ineffable, that is, beyond words. My second statement means that the sacred is ultimately Mystery (with a capital M), beyond all of our concepts and images. No language is capable of expressing the Mystery that is God.

This also is quite different from how I saw God the first time. Growing up in the church, I thought we knew quite a bit about God. After all, we had the Bible. As the Word of God, it was God's self-revelation: God had told us what God is like. We had the creeds, and the solemnity with which we stood and said them conveyed the conviction that these were statements of absolute truth about God. I thus took it for granted that we knew a lot about God and that the words we used told us with a reasonable amount of precision what God is like, for they came from God.

I now see this quite differently. I agree with those voices, ancient and modern, that emphasize that God is beyond all words and concepts.

One of my favorite expressions of this awareness is from the Tao te Ching, a classic Chinese religious text from the sixth century B.C., attributed to a sage named Lao Tzu. The word Tao is roughly the equivalent of "the sacred." The opening line of the Tao te Ching is, "The Tao that can be named is not the eternal Tao." If you can name it, if you put it into words, you are no longer talking about it. The Tao—God/the sacred—is beyond all words and names.

The same insight is affirmed in different ways in other traditions. We find it in the Jewish prohibition of graven images. This prohibition does not simply forbid statues and visual images of God; it is grounded in the conviction that no image can adequately represent God. Within the Hindu tradition with its multiplicity of gods and images of gods the opposite strategy is used to make the same point: God—the sacred—is not to be identified with any one representation of God. Islam speaks of the ninety-nine names of God, suggesting that no one name is adequate.

Affirmations of the ineffability of God continue in the modern world. Elizabeth Johnson, a brilliant contemporary Catholic feminist theologian and author of an award-winning book about God with the provocative title She Who Is, speaks of "God's hiddenness or incomprehensibility":

God's unlikeness to the finite world of matter and spirit
is total. Human beings simply cannot understand God.
No human concept, word, or image can ever circumscribe

the divine reality. Nor can any human construct express
with any measure of adequacy the mystery of God who
is ineffable.[2]

So also, Walter Brueggemann, today's best-known Christian scholar
of the Hebrew Bible. In his recent book on the theology of the Old
Testament, he refers to "the hiddenness, density and inscrutability" of
the biblical text as it speaks about God. He warns of theology's dangerous tendency to domesticate the mystery of God through "excessive certitude."[3]

The domestication of God through "excessive certitude" happens
in both conservative and liberal forms of Christian theology.
Conservative theology often domesticates the mystery of God by
claiming that we know a lot about God because God has revealed
such knowledge to us. Liberal theology has tended to domesticate the
mystery by reducing God to what makes sense within an
Enlightenment worldview.

This domestication of mystery happens in secular form, too. We
see it in the modern confidence that we basically know what "this" is
(and by "this," I mean simply what is all around us). For much of modern secularism there is no ultimate mystery, but only things we have
not figured out yet.

It seems to me that these ancient and modern voices affirming the
ineffability of God are correct. Ultimately the sacred is Mystery,
beyond all of our concepts and images. An immediate implication of
this is that all of our language about God is necessarily metaphorical
and relative, not literal and absolute. Our language about God can only
point; it cannot precisely describe.

Yet—and these voices would agree—our language about God
matters and matters greatly. For, as I emphasized in my prologue, our
language about God shapes how we see God. So I turn now to our
concepts and images of God and how they matter. Concepts concern how we see the being of God. Images concern how we see the
character of God. I will treat these separately, in my third and fourth
statements.

Our Concepts and Images of God

Our concept of God matters

I have learned that our concept of God matters. By *concept of God,* in my third statement, I mean what we think the word *God* means or refers to. When we use that word, what are we thinking of? What are we imagining? Our concept of God includes how we imagine the being of God and God's relationship to the world. To use spatial imagery, where is God in relation to the world, the universe?

In Christian history, there have been primarily two concepts of God, or two forms of theism. They are very different from each other.

The first form of theism is often called supernatural theism. This is the most common form of Christian theism, at least in the modern period. It is so common that Kenneth Leech, a contemporary Anglican theologian, speaks of it as "conventional Western theism."

Put very compactly, supernatural theism has two central features. The first: It sees God as a personlike being "out there," a being separate from the universe. The second feature is interventionism: From "out there" God occasionally intervenes within the universe.

This is the form of theism I grew up with, as did many of you, I suspect. I thought of God as a personlike being who had created the universe a long time ago as something separate from God's self. Since then, God had occasionally intervened in the universe, especially in the more dramatic events reported in the biblical tradition. Above all, this intervention had happened in Jesus. Jesus was the unique incarnation from "out there" of the God who is normally not here. From heaven above God sent his son (to use the masculine pronoun that went with God in my youth).

Throughout my childhood, I took this way of thinking about God for granted. I accepted it without difficulty. It was effortless and did not even require faith.

But the God of supernatural theism began to generate serious problems as I moved into late childhood and my teenage years. The more I learned about the enormous size of the universe, "out there" got farther and farther away, and God became more and more remote.

My prayer life was negatively affected. Increasingly, prayer seemed like trying to talk to somebody who was very far away, and even like calling into a universe that might be empty.

Moreover, the notion of supernatural intervention became more and more difficult. If God sometimes intervenes, I wondered, how can one account for the non-interventions?

To be obvious, if God could have intervened to stop the Holocaust, but chose not to, what kind of sense does that make? If God could intervene to keep an airplane from crashing but chooses not to, what kind of sense does that make?

The God of supernatural theism became harder and harder to believe in. And because it was the only way of thinking about God—the only form of theism—that I knew of, I experienced my difficulties with it as creeping atheism.

Indeed, by my twenties my creeping atheism had become full-blown closet atheism. Supernatural theism had turned me into an atheist.

Parenthetically, I add that I have since realized that there are at least two different forms of atheism. I call them absolute atheism and relative atheism. Absolute atheism is the rejection of any and all notions of God or the sacred. Relative atheism means being an atheist in relation to, that is, relative to, a particular notion of God. This distinction matters because some people who think they are "atheists" might in fact be only "relative atheists."

To illustrate: When somebody says to me, "Well, you see, I really don't believe in God," my response is, "Tell me about the God you don't believe in." Almost always, the God they do not believe in is the God of supernatural theism. That is what had happened to me. I was in fact a relative atheist, though at the time I thought I was a complete atheist. It was therefore utterly crucial in my own spiritual journey to realize that there was another way of conceptualizing God, that is, another form of theism.

It took me a long time to see this, largely because this other way of seeing God stretches the modern imagination. Indeed, it moves beyond the boundaries of modernity. In my thirties, I began to glimpse this very different way of seeing God. It came about because of a combination of religious experience and reading in areas of religious studies outside of my specialization in biblical scholarship.

Through my reading, I realized that this other form of theism was just as old and just as ancient as supernatural theism. Supernatural theism and this other way of seeing God are found side by side in the biblical tradition and in the Christian tradition from its beginnings and throughout its history. Indeed, according to Karen Armstrong's *A History of God,* these two concepts of God run side by side not only in Christianity but also in Judaism and Islam.

So what is this other concept of God? I begin with an abstract way of putting it. God or the sacred is a nonmaterial layer or level or dimension of reality, in addition to the visible world of our ordinary experience. Moreover, the sacred is not somewhere else, but all around us. God is not "out there" but "right here" (as well as more than "right here").

To use biblical language, this form of theism sees God as "the encompassing Spirit." It is the way of seeing God spoken of in Acts 17:28 in words attributed to Paul. Listen carefully to how the words work: God is "the one in whom we live and move and have our being." God is not somewhere else. God is all around us; we live and move and have our being in God. We, and everything that is, are in God.

It is the way of seeing God spoken of in Psalm 139:7–10. The author asks, "Where can I go from your Spirit?" Envisioning the whole of the three-story universe of the ancient imagination, he answers his own question: "If I ascend to heaven, you are there; if I make my bed in Sheol [the bowels of the earth], you are there. If I take the wings of the morning and settle at the farthest limits of the sea, even there your hand shall lead me." Wherever he goes, God is there. How is that possible? Because we are in God, and there is no place we can be and be outside God.

The same way of seeing God is suggested by the meanings of the biblical words for "spirit." In both Hebrew (*ruach*) and Greek (*pneuma*), the words that we translate as "spirit" also mean "wind" and "breath." The Spirit—God—is like wind and breath.

Think of what "wind" was to ancient people. I doubt that they thought of the wind as molecules in motion. Rather, they would have experienced the wind as a nonmaterial and nonvisible reality that was nevertheless manifestly real and had effects. And breath was the life force within us; when it is gone, life is gone. And so Spirit— God, the sacred—is the wind that moves outside us and is the breath that moves within us. God is a nonmaterial reality around us and within us.

This form of theism is commonly called *panentheism*. Panentheism (with its middle syllable *en*) is very different from pantheism, with which it is often confused. Its Greek roots indicate the meaning of panentheism. The first syllable *pan* means "all" or "everything." The middle syllable *en* is a Greek preposition meaning "in." Theism, of course, is from the Greek word for God, *theos*. So panentheism means "everything is in God."

Sometimes this form of theism is called *dialectical theism*. Dialectical theism affirms two claims about God deeply rooted in the biblical and Christian traditions and shared in common with most of the world's religions; namely, that God or the sacred is both transcendent and immanent.

Transcendence and *immanence* are semitechnical terms. To transcend means to go beyond. The transcendence of God thus refers to God's "beyondness" and "otherness" and "moreness." To be immanent means "to dwell within." The immanence of God thus refers to God's "hereness" and "nearness."

Dialectical theism is a form of theism that affirms both God's transcendence and God's immanence. God is both beyond us, even as God is among us; God is both "here" and "more than right here." Dialectical theism and panentheism are thus two different terms for the same concept of God: We are in God (and thus God is "right here"), even as God is "more" than right here.

To use the language of transcendence and immanence to summarize the difference between the two forms of Christian theism:

Supernatural theism emphasizes only the transcendence of God (the "moreness" or "beyondness" of God) and thus sees God as "out there."

Panentheism, or dialectical theism, emphasizes both transcendence and immanence and thus sees God as "right here" (immanent) as well as "more than right here" (transcendent).

Whether we call it *panentheism* or *dialectical theism* or something else is unimportant. What is important is to understand the notion, this second form of theism.

I am a strong advocate of this second concept of God with its robust affirmation of both transcendence and immanence. There are three compelling reasons. First, it is intellectually far more satisfactory than supernatural theism; it does not create the problems that supernatural theism does. Second, it is biblical as well as orthodox Christianity—orthodox, because it affirms both the transcendence and immanence of God. Supernatural theism as an ontological claim is modern, not ancient. It is the result of emphasizing the transcendence of God to the exclusion of immanence, a development that began in the Enlightenment.

Third and finally, I affirm this form of theism because of the evidence from religious experience. Throughout human history, in virtually every culture known to us, people have had experiences that have seemed to them overwhelmingly to be experiences of the sacred. I take such experiences very seriously. Indeed, if God is not an experiential reality, then the notion of God remains a hypothesis and not a very persuasive one at that. And if God can be experienced, then God is in some sense "right here," accessible, all around us, as well as more than right here.

To make the transition to my fourth statement: What is this God like? What is the "character" of this God? The answer lies in our image of God.

The "Character" of God

How we image God matters

I have learned that how we image God matters. I begin my fourth statement by making a distinction between images of God and concepts of

God. I think of images of God as more visual, more "concrete," and concepts as more abstract.

To put that slightly differently, an image of God is a metaphor. Some of the biblical metaphors for God include these: God is like a king, like a judge, like a shepherd, like a father, like a mother, like a lover, like a potter, like a warrior, and so forth. Metaphors are linguistic art or verbal art.

Most importantly, our images of God—our metaphors for God—matter because they shape how we see the character of God. Character has to do with the very nature of God. It is deeper than the will of God, for will flows out of character. And so the crucial question is, as the contemporary Jesus scholar John Dominic Crossan vividly and provocatively puts it, "What is the character of your God?" What is God's character? What does God care about? What is God's passion?

Within the Christian tradition, there are two primary and yet very different "models" for the character of God. A "model," as the contemporary theologian Sallie McFague puts it, is a metaphor with staying power.[4] To which I would add that a model is a way of constellating or "gestalting" metaphors. The biblical metaphors for God gravitate toward one or the other of these two models.

Different models for imaging God

I turn to comparing and contrasting two very different models for imaging the character of God. Both have been present throughout Christian history, and both are alive in the contemporary church. They are so different that they virtually produce two different religions, both using the same language.

For the first image, I turn once again to "how I saw God the first time." The primary image of God with which I grew up was an image of God as a lawgiver and judge who also loved us.

As lawgiver, God had given us the Ten Commandments and other laws about how to live. God had told us what is expected of us. As judge, God was the enforcer of law. There would be a judgment some day. Because we were not very good at keeping God's law, we deserved judgment.

But God also loved us. So God had provided an alternative means of satisfying God's law and becoming right with God. In Old Testament times, this was accomplished through temple sacrifice as a way of atoning for our disobedience. In New Testament times, God sent Jesus as the Son of God to be the sacrifice by dying for our sins, thus making our forgiveness possible.

So God did love us—but it was a conditional love. God would accept us if our repentance was earnest and if we believed in Jesus. Thus the system of requirements remained. The dynamic of sin, guilt, and forgiveness, and of doing or believing what we needed to, was the central dynamic of the Christian life.

I have since learned to call this way of imaging God's character "the monarchical model" of God, a phrase I owe to Ian Barbour and Sallie McFague. It draws its name from the common biblical metaphor of God as "king" and "Lord." As king, God is both lawgiver and judge—and we don't measure up very well.

This model is softened somewhat (but not much) when parental imagery (usually "father") is substituted for king imagery. When we image the monarchical God as a parent rather than as a king, it is as the critical parent. God becomes the disappointed parent—the parent who loves us, yes, but on the whole is not all that pleased with how we have turned out. God functions as a divine superego in our heads, a voice that ranges and rages along a spectrum from "You're never quite good enough" to "You're no good."

The monarchical model   Imaging God's character with the monarchical model has a number of consequences. I will mention four:

First, and to say the obvious, the monarchical God is a God of requirements. It suggests that the Christian life is about measuring up and doing or believing what God requires of us.

Second, it leads to an in-group and out-group distinction. There are those who do measure up and those who do not, those who are saved and those who are not.

Third, ultimately the monarchical God is a God of vengeance. The internal logic of the model is clear: God is going to "get" all of those people who do not measure up, who do not meet the requirements. There will be a judgment, either after death with the prospect of heaven or hell, or at the second coming. To cite Crossan again, most Christian visions of the second coming see it as "divine ethnic cleansing." God is going to get all of those people who are not like us.

Fourth and finally, this God does not liberate us from self-preoccupation. Rather, this God focuses our attention on our own salvation and on making sure that we have done or believed what is necessary. We remain preoccupied with ourselves.

The "divine lover" model   I turn now to the second primary model for imaging God's character. To give it a shorthand label, I call it the "divine lover" model.

The image of God as lover is deeply rooted in the biblical tradition. It occurs frequently in the prophets of the Hebrew Bible. To cite just one example: in Isa. 43:4f, the prophet says, in the name of God, to the Jewish people in exile: "You are precious in my sight, and honored, and I love you . . . . Do not fear."

God as lover is the central image in the Song of Solomon, that collection of erotic love poetry also known as the Song of Songs (a phrase that means "the best song"). Understood by Jews and Christians alike as an allegory of divine love, this was the single most popular biblical book among Christians of the Middle Ages.

The image of God as lover is also widespread in the New Testament. It is found in its bestknown verse, John 3:16, which begins, "For God so loved the world." Jesus is here seen as the embodiment or incarnation of God as lover.

To image God as lover changes the dynamic of the Christian life. God is in love with us. We are precious in God's eyes and honored. God yearns for us. As the contemporary scholar of early Christian spirituality Roberta Bondi so compactly puts it, "God is besotted with us." [5]

For just a moment, think of the difference it would make in your life if you knew, at the deepest level of your being, that God is besotted with you and yearns for you. The effect is very different from the monarchical model. The monarchical model puts us on guard: There are requirements to be met, rewards and punishments to be considered. But the divine lover model changes the way we see the character of God. Rather than God being the one we need to please, whether through good deeds or earnest repentance and faith, God as lover is passionate about us and yearns to be in a relationship with us.

There is a danger in the divine lover model. The danger is that it can become too individualistic and too "sweet," as if it meant primarily that God loves me. But the image of God as lover means that God loves everybody—not just me and not just us, but everybody. So the image of God as lover is very much associated with the concreteness and particularity of life in this world.

As lover, God is liberator. This is the central theme of the most important story that ancient Israel knew, the story of the exodus from Egypt: liberation from an oppression that was simultaneously economic, political, and religious. Images of God as liberator continue through Israel's history and into the New Testament. It is not God's will that we be in bondage, whether internally or externally.

As lover, God is compassionate. The model of God as lover sees God's character as compassionate. As many of you know, compassion is an unusually rich metaphor in the Bible, related to the word for womb. To say that God's character is compassion is to say that God is "like a womb" or "womblike": life-giving, nourishing.

Compassion also has a resonance associated with the feeling that a mother has for the children of her womb.

What do these feelings include? Tenderness. Willing their well-being. Hope. Concern. Importantly, feelings "from the womb" are not simply "soft." They can become fierce, as when a mother sees the children of her womb threatened or treated dreadfully.

To apply the metaphor: Just as a mother feels compassion for her children and wills their well-being and can become fierce in the defense of her children, so God feels compassion for her children, and wills their well-being, and can become fierce in the defense of her children, all of her children.

And so, as lover, God is not only compassionate but also passionate about social justice. God as lover is passionate about social justice for the simple reason that its opposite, systemic injustice, is the single greatest source of unnecessary human suffering and misery in history.

Social justice is the way human well-being is attained.

God as lover is in love not only with us as human beings, but also with the nonhuman world, the whole of creation. Thus, both a passion for justice and a passion for the environment flow out of imaging God as lover.

To bring this section to a close: Depending upon which of these models we emphasize, we will see the character of God very differently. We will see the Christian life in very different ways. Is it about meeting requirements for individual salvation? Or is it about a relationship with God the lover?

The ethical imperative that goes with each is quite different. For the monarchical model the ethical imperative is "Be good, because you will be called to account; there will be a judgment." For the divine lover model the ethical imperative is "Love that which God loves." So, "What is the character of your God?"

How We "See" Reality

God is real

My fifth statement is brief, but no less important for its brevity. I have learned that God is real. As you know from earlier in this talk, there was a time when I was not at all sure about this. Indeed, I was relatively sure that God was not real. The God who I thought was not real was the God of supernatural theism. Thus I tried to believe in a God whose reality seemed doubtful to me.

Now, it seems obvious to me that God or the sacred is. This is not something I can demonstrate. But there are moments when we "see" this. In moments of "radical amazement," to use a favorite phrase from Abraham Heschel, when the domestications of reality in our words, concepts, and categories fall away, we behold the Mystery. These are moments when, to use a biblical phrase, we see "the whole earth filled with the glory or radiant presence of God."

In moments like these, as Heschel puts it, even the statement "God is" is an understatement. If, when we use the word "God," we are thinking of a reality who may or may not exist, then we are not thinking of God.

In short, the question of God is not about the existence of another being, but the question of how we "see" reality. By reality, I mean, "What is this that is all around us, "the whole?" We may see it as ordinary, as nothing special or as simply a whirling collocation of matter and energy. Or we may see it as wondrous and amazing, life-giving and nourishing, beyond all of our explanations, to which the appropriate response is awe, gratitude, and doxology.

Not believing but living in relationship

This leads to my sixth and final statement. I have learned that life with God, whether in its Christian form or some other form, is not very much about believing in God but about living in relationship with God.

The notion that Christian faith is about "believing" is a modern development and a distortion of faith. It is the product of the Enlightenment's challenge to Christianity and religion. In the period of the Enlightenment many traditional Christian teachings became doubtful, and Christian faith meant believing these teachings to be true in spite of their doubtful status. Not only is this an odd notion of faith but it also puts the emphasis in the wrong place. Believing is relatively impotent. You can believe all the right things and still be a jerk, or still be in bondage, or still be miserable.

I have become convinced that the Christian life is not about believing or about requirements. Rather, it is about our relationship with the Mystery in whom we live and move and have our being, with the one to whom the Christian tradition and all of the enduring religious traditions point. The Christian life is not about believing in the Christian tradition, but about a relationship to God lived within the framework of the Christian tradition, just as being Jewish or Muslim is about a relationship with God lived within the framework of those traditions. The religious life is thus about a deepening relationship with the God who is known by many names, the one who is right here as well as more than right here.

Follow-up Questions

MB = Marcus Borg   Q = Questioner   M = Moderator

M   Marcus, let me ask you a question. You use words that are very foreign to us Westerners. Like hiddenness, and incomprehensibility, and ineffability, and inscrutability. We've thought for centuries now that the ideal for us was to be certain, not in doubt. In a sense, it's a new language that you're introducing, new words, new ways of thinking. Do you see it as that kind of major transformation?

MB Your way of phrasing the question is very interesting. I see these as very ancient notions, not modern. But you're absolutely on target. These notions are quite foreign to the spirit of modernity, which is shorthand for the understanding that emerged in the Enlightenment. During the period of modernity, the conflict between religion and science was very intense. It was a conflict between religion and the quest for certitude. What's interesting about talking about God at 2000 is that the conflict between religion and science has significantly changed. Because of developments in science, post-modern science is much more comfortable with metaphor and uncertainty, and with language that can only point, rather than precisely describe. So the notions of incomprehensibility and ineffability are both very ancient and very contemporary. Post-modern science and religion share in common the awareness that, in some fundamental sense, we don't know what this— this that is all around us—is.

Q   I think a lot of people wonder where the God of love was during the 20th century. The Holocaust was only one portion of the horrors of the 20th century. There are many, many more.

If the God of love was around, that God seemed to be very impotent.

MB Your question is extremely important. My basic response is that the events of the 20th century and similar events of previous centuries make utterly impossible the belief in an interventionist God. Now, I don't mean that God is absent, like the deist God of some Enlightenment thinkers. Rather, I think God is right here and involved in the process, present with us even in our suffering. I don't think of God as a cause operating in the world alongside of other causes. Letting go of interventionism doesn't make the Holocaust any less terrible, of course. Letting go of interventionism does mean that terrible events like that do not count against the reality of God. The God of love is present with us in our suffering, but can't get us off the hook by just "zapping" in. I do think that paranormal healings happen, but I don't want to go down that road just now. Rather, my denial is specifically a denial of the notion of intervention.

Q We had the curious thing of Christian nations killing other Christians and warring with other Christian nations. We see this over and over again—each one thinking they're right.

MB Religion and religious people are not exempt from the blindness that so often characterizes human existence.

Q I'm wondering how and when our language will catch up with the inclusiveness of he/she/them, the "bigness" of life.

MB Are you thinking of gender-inclusive language in particular?

Q Yes, but there's more.

MB It's real different now than it was even twenty-five years ago. It is now unusual, in the United States, to find a book published in religious studies that does not use inclusive language. Most now use gender inclusive language. On the level of popular usage, progress is slower. Some people think inclusive language is simply a matter of political correctness. I find that many of my under-

graduates still tend to use non-inclusive language, so I correct
them. Beyond that, I'm very hopeful about what I see in major
portions of the mainline church. Not only is there a sensitivity
to gender language, but a growing awareness that the Christian
language system itself is one relative language system in a world
of pluralistic language systems. So I think it's happening.

Q Giving up one image of God and moving to another is kind of
like swinging on a trapeze, and sometimes I feel like I'm in the
middle. I've let go of the old image, but I don't really know what
I'm grabbing hold of. You mentioned that images are more visual,
and that concepts are more abstract. I'm wrestling with—and I
know a lot of people are—the idea of the evolving universe of
the new creation story, and thus of a God that is not so anthropomorphic. Can you provide any help with visual images that
feed and nurture that in prayer and worship?

MB I had to make lots of decisions about what to leave out in a relatively brief lecture. So I left out a section on non-anthropomorphic ways of imaging God in the biblical tradition itself. I
did briefly mention God as "spirit," which means both wind and
breath: God as the wind outside of us, as well as the breath within
us. But there are many more non-anthropomorphic images of
God, such as fire and light. I am very struck myself by Sallie
McFague's image of the universe as the body of God. It is a nice
organic metaphor: God is the animating spirit that enlivens the
universe as God's body. So there are images that move us beyond
God as a person-like being more in touch with the earth and the
universe without losing the quality of "presence."

Q Good morning. I'm calling from Texas. I'd like to know if the hope
of a relationship with God exists only among monotheistic people. I noticed that you gave only examples from the monotheistic
religions when you spoke of the relationship with God. And a second part of my question: Do monotheistic believers have any possibility of a spiritual connection to polytheistic believers?

MB I know the Western religious traditions better than I know other religions. So I can't speak with as much confidence about them. But my impression is that in a number of Asian traditions, including Buddhism and Hinduism, there are forms of theism that are very similar to Western notions of monotheism, even though there is also denial of theism in some forms of Buddhism. Buddhists themselves disagree about how much of this difference is difference in language, and how much of it involves a difference in ontological claim. But if you think of the question of "the sacred" as the question of how you see reality, then I think what I'm saying would apply to Asian religious traditions as well as to Western ones.

M From Chapel Hill, North Carolina, a question. Are the monarchical and divine lover models mutually exclusive? Can't they co-exist and be blended in some way?

MB Yes and no. Some people do affirm both, but it seems that one will always be subordinated to the other. In my own growing up experience, both were present. We knew that God loved us. John 3:16—"For God so loved the world"—was the first Bible verse I memorized. But it was also very clear that there were requirements. You had to be a Christian. You had to earnestly repent. There were conditions on God's love. So even though both images were there, God as lover was subordinated to God as lawgiver and judge. Now let me add an important qualification. The story of God as divine lover can be told in such a way that it ultimately subverts God the lawgiver and judge. I think this was Martin Luther's personal religious experience; his deep anxiety about God as lawgiver and judge was broken through his experience of God as lover. I think this is the way the image of Jesus as the sacrifice for sin properly works. I don't take that story literally, but its metaphorical meaning is powerful. If Jesus is the sacrifice for sin sent by God, it means that God has undermined and subverted the whole system of requirements. The story uses the language of God as lawgiver and judge to undermine the image of God as lawgiver and judge. But simply to affirm both the monarchical and lover models without thinking through their logic usually ends up in a conditional form of love. And a conditional form of love is a terrible form of love. Well, maybe I'd rather have a conditional form of love than no love at all. But you've always got to worry about losing it.

Q I'm calling from Rhode Island. Let's start with the scientific premise that energy can neither be created nor destroyed, but merely changed in form. If we use that metaphor for our existence in relationship with God across all of the Abrahamic religions, then cannot we see that Christ came to save us, to show us all that preceded him, all the laws of the Old Testament, were really directives to teach us that we have to be in relationship? And his example was to show us what that perfect relationship can be.

MB I like where you ended, but I'm not sure how you got there. I'm struggling to see the connection to your premise about the conservation of matter and energy. So let me just say "Amen" to where you ended.

Q My question has to do with the lover and monarchical models of God. You used the first half of John 3:16, "For God so loved the world." But if you deal with the second half of the verse and verses seventeen and eighteen, doesn't that bring back the monarchical view? And then, quickly, about your sixth statement—that Christianity is not very much about believing but about a relationship. How do you deal with the emphasis of verse sixteen on believing?

MB The key, I think, is the meaning of the word "believe." In the biblical tradition, the word we translate "believe" often does not mean "accept as true," as if believing were about giving your mental assent to a statement. Rather, in the Bible, "believe" often means "give your heart to," a metaphor for giving the self at its deepest level to God. So the meaning of "believe" in John 3:16 is very different from, "If you believe all of this to be true, you'll be saved." It means something like, "Whoever gives his or her heart to Jesus as the decisive disclosure of God will be transformed." One further comment: it's important to note how our model for thinking about God's character affects how we hear or read particular verses. Earlier in my life, for example, I heard John 3:16 within the framework of the monarchical model: God "gave" Jesus for the sins of the world. But I now realize that this verse says nothing at all about Jesus dying for the sins of the world. Rather, it sees Jesus as the expression of God's love.

Q I'm familiar with Whitehead and his "process" understanding of God, and I'm becoming a little bit familiar with Tillich and his notion of God as "the ground of being." Is this like what you're talking about, and are there other writers I could read?

MB Yes. They're very much in the same ballpark. Whitehead is brilliant, and his understanding is consistent with what I have talked about today, but his language and metaphors have never resonated very strongly with me. I have learned much from Tillich and see him as a pantheistic thinker, but God as "the ground of being" has always struck me as a rather colorless phrase. I think John Cobb is the contemporary process theologian whose writing is most accessible, plus Sallie McFague's books *Models of God* and *The Body of God*.

Q You have spoken about a relationship to God as a relationship to "what is." What function do your religious beliefs and practices have as you try to relate to "what is" in your everyday life?

MB I love the question. I have a number of comments. First, I think religious traditions originate as responses to the experience of the sacred. Second, what is their function for us? To use a phrase from Huston Smith, religious traditions are the way that "spirituality gets traction within history" and survives from one generation to another. Even more importantly, I see religious traditions, including Christianity and the Bible, as sacraments of the sacred. I'm using language very precisely here. A sacrament is a mediator of the sacred, a means whereby the sacred comes to us. To say that a religious tradition is a sacrament of the sacred is to say, "It's not something to be believed in." Rather, you are to live within the tradition and let it do its work of mediating the sacred. This is also the purpose of most religious practices: Prayer in its many forms, worship, pilgrimage, solitude, even fasting. All of these are ways of opening our hearts—our selves at their deepest level—to the reality of God. The title of a lecture that I have given several times this year expresses the purpose of religion well: "Open Hearts and Thin Places." Religious traditions and practices are to become "thin places" where our hearts are opened to the reality of the sacred.

Q   My question is on prayer. If God is non-interventionist, what is the purpose of prayer? Does God respond?

MB   I think prayer has many purposes within a non-interventionist model. Let me begin with what seems like the most problematic kind of prayer, intercessory prayer. I practice intercessory prayer myself: I pray for my family's health and safety, for friends, for somebody I know who is suffering, and for the general suffering of the world. For me to refuse to do intercessory prayer because I don't believe in interventionism would be to claim to know too much. It would imply that the only way God can act is through intervention. But I don't know that. There may well be non-interventionist ways in which God is involved in the process. I think paranormal healings happen, and I think they sometimes happen in response to prayer. But I refuse to use interventionism as the explanation, just as I refuse to use psychosomatic explanations. Both explanations claim to know too much. So I do intercessory prayer because it seems like a natural act of caring, and because refusing to do so because I can't imagine the explanatory mechanism would be an act of intellectual arrogance. The other forms of prayer fit very well, especially contemplative prayer, which is a way of becoming still and quiet inside and opening one's self to the reality that is all around us. Even daily conversational prayer is a way of addressing the reality all around us as a "you." And I find that on days when I remember to do this, my life goes better. Experience reality as a "you."

2 Honest to God: The Universe of Faith
Diana Eck

Diana Eck teaches at Harvard Divinity School and Harvard University, where she is Professor of Comparative Religions and Indian Studies. A well-known award-winning author and scholar of religions in India, she is deeply involved in the study of religious pluralism and the practice of interreligious dialogue.

Her books include: *Banaras: City of Light; Darsan: Seeing the Divine Image in India; Speaking of Faith: Global Perspectives on Women, Religion, and Social Change* (edited with Devaki Jain); *Devotion Divine: Bhakti Traditions from the Regions of India* (edited with Francoise Mallison); and *Encountering God: A Spiritual Journey from Bozeman to Banaras.* Eck was winner of the 1994 Melcher Book Award and the 1995 Louisville Grawemeyer Book Award in Religion, seen by many as the most prestigious book award in the field of religious studies.

As a scholar of religious pluralism and diversity, Eck has worked closely with churches, including her own United Methodist Church and the World Council of Churches.

Since 1991 she has been the director of the Pluralism Project, whose task has been the study of the growing presence in the United States of Muslim, Buddhist, Hindu, Sikh, Jain, and Zoroastrian communities. The Pluralism Project has received grants from the Lilly Endowment, the Pew Charitable Trusts, and the Ford Foundation. The Project's interactive multimedia CD-ROM, *On Common Ground: World Religions in America*, was published in 1997.

In 1998, Professor Eck was awarded the National Humanities Medal by President Clinton for her leadership of the Pluralism Project.

Eck grew up in Montana. She received her bachelor's degree from Smith College, her master's from the University of London, and her doctorate from Harvard.

I, for one, was thrilled at the dawning of the new millennium. I was not a skeptic. I did not stay at home. I both watched televised celebrations and waded out into the throngs of Boston revelers. I did my share of rejoicing and bell ringing, all the while thinking about religion, technology, and the new and old world in which we live. The millennium was not only a moment in time, but also a worldwide televised "production"—from the dawning of the century's first sunlight in New Zealand, greeted by Maori dancers, to the last splash of fireworks in the skies of Hawaii. Around the world we saw the festivities as the cycle of fireworks exploded into the night sky in Sydney, New Delhi, Bethlehem, and Paris. As I stood with my mother and our gathered family on the Boston Common for the early "family fireworks" display at 7:00 P.M. on December 31, we watched as huge outdoor video screens brought us the festivities live from the Millennium Dome in London. The simultaneity rendered by our technology linked us Boston Common revelers with Queen Elizabeth in the United Kingdom.

Calling on God in a Thousand Names

As the fireworks began and I felt the thunder of the explosions on my chest, I could not help thinking how the globalization of our technology, communications, financial markets, and businesses stood in sobering contrast to the deep fracturing of the human community caused by old and new religious identities and rivalries. Even as the new millennium was dawning, we human beings were enacting our age-old struggles and rivalries, claiming divine truth for our own partisans and employing the full arsenal of religious symbols to protect it. In my mind's eye I could imagine us all, the vast human family, invoking, praising, and petitioning divinity in a thousand names and languages: lifting our prayers this day at the Western Wall in Jerusalem, at the Dome of the Rock and at the Holy Sepulchre; offering prayers in the little shrine designated as the birthplace of Krishna in Mathura, India, and directly above it, in the mosque built on that very site; bowing for prayers in the mosques of Kosovo and in the churches of Belgrade. Multifaith services, I reflected, would be held, like the one at midnight at St. Paul's Cathedral, on the edge of the Boston Common. We would gather together to hear one another in prayer and praise. Religiously speaking, as the year 2000 was about to break upon us, it was business as usual. Our communities of faith are still struggling to provide visionary leadership in the new era that is dawning.

The sheer volume of prayers uttered around the globe should give us pause to think about our God-language. Our communication satellites can circle the globe, but why is our understanding of the central symbols of our faith so provincial and territorial? We implore God for protection and success on both sides of partisan causes and ancient rivalries. We invoke God both to judge and to succor people with AIDS, both to save our children and homes from the sinful encroachment of homosexuality and to save our same-sex households from the hatred of homophobia. We speak of God in splendid churches even as we see the chasm between the rich and the poor deepen and widen. How can we sustain our faith in a world where the wealthiest twenty percent control eighty-six percent of the world's product, while the poorest twenty percent are left out of the growth of globalization entirely? How do we relate our faith and our faith communities to a world of millions of refugees, orphans, and new millionaires? Is this the God to whom we all pray, the recipient of such a Babel of tongues?

The reality that we cannot grasp

As a Christian, I begin my reflections on "God at 2000" with the simple insistence that the one we Christians call God is not ours.

Whatever this word *God* points toward is greater than our understanding and greater than everything we think we mean. God transcends our understanding of what that word *God* means. That should
be the source of deep religious humility on our part. Our compass
and guide is this: to know that the most important thing for us to
know is what we cannot fully know.

As a scholar of religion, I can report that every tradition makes this
clear in one way or another. Those of us who are Christians evoke the
complexity and mystery of God with the language of the Trinity. Jews
do not write out the word *God*, the Holy One, the "I am" who spoke
to Moses out of a burning bush. Muslims do not image God in any
human form, indeed in any form at all. Hindus speak of 330 million
gods, which amounts to the same thing. The sage of Ecclesiastes suggests the irony of our dilemma when he writes, "God has put a sense
of past and future into their minds, yet they cannot find out what God
has done from the beginning to the end." (Eccl. 3.11) As the Taittiriya
Upanishad puts it, the ultimate reality is that "whence mind and
speech, having no hold, fall back."[6]

Many Buddhists do not use the language of "God" at all, but speak
only of the "far shore," the reality that we cannot grasp but may awaken
to. In the Dalai Lama's book *Ethics for a New Millennium,* His Holiness
writes powerfully on the challenges confronting our world today without ever employing the word *God*. He speaks directly to the spiritual
challenges of our inner lives today, yet without reference to the word
that has gathered us here. The Buddhist poet and philosopher Thich
Nhat Hanh has written, "Discussing God is not the best use of our
energy."[7] We can see the point, perhaps readily.

God is surely one of the most used and abused words in the
English language. I typed the three letters "G-o-d" into my Internet
search engine and got over four million web pages that had some reference to God. Yet, finally, I disagree with Thich Nhat Hanh. I *do*
think discussing God is a good use of our energy, at least for those of
us who use this word and mean something ultimate in our use of it.
As long as some of us in our respective families of faith continue to

pour forth speech about God—about what God has given, does and should do, wills and does not will—we must discuss God. We are responsible for our use and abuse of this language. God is not ours, but we are responsible for the ways in which we speak of God. We are accountable for the human language we formulate to express what we cannot fully comprehend. We are responsible when our God-talk becomes idolatrous.

Families of Faith: Sharing a Common World

Forty years ago when Bishop John A.T. Robinson wrote *Honest to God,* he spoke out of a deep need to be utterly honest—to himself and to God. He wrestled with the revolutions of modernity and scientific knowledge. He saw that our religious worldview requires refashioning as scientists explore the black holes of the heavens and chart the intricacies of the human genome. If "God" for us is merely the answer to all that we cannot understand, we human beings will be left with a God who reigns over the remainder, whatever is left over after science has done its work. Our God will be increasingly underemployed as one mystery after another is accounted for. Science has made us come to grips with an overly anthropomorphic idea of a God who tinkers from the heavens with the world he has made. Honest theologians like Robinson and Paul Tillich launched a new kind of God-language. If we are to think of God in the highest heavens, we must also think of God in the depths of our being. God is not in this direction or that, up or down, out there or in here. God is a dimension of our being both in its depth and its expansive breadth.

My own "honest to God" question

I read *Honest to God* with eagerness and gratefulness as a college student, but my own "honest to God" question today is a different one from that posed by Robinson. It is shaped not so much by modernity and science but by our encounter with people of other faiths. My question is: How do we who are followers of Christ think about God in the world we now know, a world of religious diversity and difference where people of other traditions of faith are no longer metaphorical neighbors around the world but neighbors across the street and across the hall? Do we imagine we are the only ones who have sought God passionately, or who have let our souls take root in the depth and loving nurture of God, or who have lived our lives and died our deaths in terms of it? What does the growing dialogue of people of many faiths have to do with our faith as Christians? This is a question that will not go away. It is not a question only for people like me who make a vocation of studying religious communities on the other side of the world. It is a question that makes theologians of us all. It makes us think anew about God. People of other religious traditions pose the same question in different ways.

Learning the language of others

If we open our eyes and ears, we come to see that there are many other ways of thinking theologically than the one we know as Christians. We discover within other faiths ways of understanding and relating to God that have all the subtlety, diversity, and intricate argumentation that has been part of our Christian tradition. Our task is to remain open to what we may learn of God in the light of what that one has been doing in the lives and hearts of other families of faith. If we understand God to be the one to whom we testify—the creator of heaven and earth and all that is within it—then what has God been doing in the lives and hearts of our neighbors of other faiths? If we understand God to be the one who was and is at work in Christ, present to us in the neighbor, the prisoner, the poor, and the stranger whom we meet on the road to Emmaus, then what may we come to know of Christ in the neighbors and strangers of our lives? If we understand God to be the Holy Spirit, blowing like the wind and sailing like the dove, how do we apprehend the spirit of God beyond the walls of the churches and communities we know best? To carry this question with us, as I have carried it with me, may not only help us understand our neighbors but also help us better understand ourselves and deepen and widen our understanding of God. The many families of faith increasingly share a common world, but we do not share a common language. By this I mean not English, French, Chinese, or Hindi, but rather the language of faith by which we live our lives. We will never all speak the same language of faith. Nor should we. That is not the goal. The challenge is to begin to learn the language of others, so that we can discern what we share in common and see more clearly what we do not share. In matters of religion there is no simultaneous translation by which I say "God," and in the earphones of others it becomes "*Allah*," "Vishnu," "Kali," or "Amitabha." These are not the same, nor are they totally different. Each is an entry point into a complex way of envisioning reality. Each contains within itself a multitude of names and attributes: the ninety-nine beautiful names of *Allah*, the thousand names of Vishnu, or the thousand names of Kali. As a Christian and as a scholar of the history of religions, I use the English word *God* so commonly and in so many different ways. I am constantly engaged in implicit and explicit commentary. I use *God* at the table before meals as the source of life to whom I express my thanks. I sing of *God* with a full heart when I sing my favorite Methodist hymns, calling on God as rock and shepherd, savior and child, shelter and eternal home, light inexpressible and bread of heaven. I use the term in class as I speak of the gods of Hindu tradition or of God in the Islamic tradition. Without an explicit recitation of the ninety-nine or thousand names of God, I already speak the name in a multitude of ways.

So on occasions like this, which are far too few in our common life, all of us must wrestle with the problem of language and the challenges of translation, posing together the questions, "What do I mean? What do you mean?" Discussing "God" together as Christians, Jews, and Muslims is a good use of our energies, for we must move from an era of competitive theisms to an era of dialogical multitheism, recognizing that our languages for God, our "theisms," are many.

Speaking as a Christian, let me say plainly that we Christians have to catch up spiritually and theologically with the dynamism of our age. We cannot enter the 21st century with ideas of God learned in Sunday school fifty years ago. We cannot live in a world in which our economies and markets are global, our political awareness is global, our business relationships take us to every continent, and the Internet connects us with colleagues half a world away, and yet live on Friday, Saturday, or Sunday with ideas of God that are essentially provincial. We cannot imagine that somehow God has been concerned primarily with our tribe and us. No one would dream of operating in the business or political world with ideas about Russia, India, or China that were formed fifty, a hundred, or five hundred years ago. The same is true for our religious and spiritual lives. I sing, "Give me that old-time religion! It's good enough for me!" with as much gusto as anyone. But in my heart of hearts I know that the old-time religion is not good enough unless those of us who claim it are able to grapple honestly and faithfully with the new questions, challenges, and knowledge presented to us by the vibrant world of many living faiths. To be good enough the old-time religion has to address the questions of an intricately interdependent world.

Three Stops on the Way

I have thought about these questions day to day for all of my adult life. So I want to take you along with me as I focus simply on the ways in which they came up in my own life during the month of January 2000. I will make three stops on the way.

Epiphany at Memorial Church, Harvard Yard

Our first stop is a glorious, sunny, and freezing-cold Sunday morning in Cambridge, Massachusetts. It was the celebration of Epiphany. As I settled into the cushioned pew at the Memorial Church in Harvard Yard, I was immersed in the language I have grown up with and have come to know through more than fifty years of formation as a

Christian. We sang, "O God, my faithful God, True fountain ever flowing, Without whom nothing is, All perfect gifts bestowing." We stood for Psalm 91 and said together, "He will cover you with his pinions, and under his wings you will find refuge."

I began thinking about this conference and noted, as the words of our service of worship unfolded, how readily we as Christians gather the image and poetry of life itself into our image of God: the flowing fountain or the broad-winged bird, covering us with its gentle feathers. We can all add our favorites to these images. God is the rock beneath our feet, the light upon our path, the shepherd who seeks us when we are lost. Our God language is as broad and rich as language itself. Using the language of the Trinity, we speak of the God who created the heavens and earth and all that is therein, who is present with us in the life of Christ, and who inspires us in the Holy Spirit. This is the God whom we can image only in the language of one who breathes within us even when we are not aware. This is the language that has come to us through the whole history of our tradition, a stream of living images and poetry that opens our eyes and hearts to the width and breadth, the height and depth, of God.

There was Holy Communion that Epiphany morning. The bread and the wine became for us the living symbol of Christ and of the community we all share in which I have grown over the years as a Christian. It constitutes, in the largest sense, my family. This is the language I speak, the story I tell, and the argument in which I participate. It is not the only family, language, story, or argument going on. But it is mine and I love it. I willingly, gratefully, and argumentatively place myself within it.

Leylat al-Qadr, the Night of Power

My second stop was a few days later on the Muslim holy day of Leylat al-Qadr, the twenty-seventh of the month of Ramadan. Leylat al-Qadr is called the Night of Power, the night when Muslims observe the revelation of the Qur'an to the Prophet Muhammad. They gather in mosques to pray and to hear these revealing words, perhaps to spend the entire night reading the Qur'an. I had been a guest in the Muslim community twice on this night. Two years previously some Muslim friends had invited me to the Islamic Center of New England in the Boston suburb of Sharon, and last year a Muslim colleague invited me to accompany her to the mosque nearby on Prospect Street in Cambridge.

The year 2000 was different. In the past six months my partner and I have taken into our home in the Masters' Residence of Lowell House at Harvard University a family of four young Kosovar refugees, teenagers who have lost both parents. Their father, a doctor, was killed before their very eyes by masked Serbian paramilitaries. They are Muslims. As the month of Ramadan began that year, I saw this month of fasting from dawn to dusk up close for the first time. In anticipating the beginning of Ramadan I had imagined that we would all get up early in the morning for a predawn breakfast. Amella and Aida, Sokol and Kreshnik had a different family custom. They are teenagers and not early risers, so their way of observance was to stay up late, watching movies until midnight, and then to have some scrambled eggs or waffles. After that, nothing. When they got up for school the next morning, they would neither drink nor eat until late afternoon. Just after sunset they would break the fast by eating the traditional dates and drinking a big glass of water. These young people do not think of themselves as particularly religious, but their unassuming faithfulness was beautiful to see. It was the Epiphany season for us. The challenge for us was to discern how to accompany these Muslim young people on their own wavelength of observance and how to support them as Muslims in an observance authentically theirs, as we kept traditions authentically ours.

As the end of the month and the Night of Power approached, the youngsters wanted to go to a mosque. During the past year the mosque on Prospect Street had grown quickly and was already far too small for the Muslim community that gathered there. So the Night of Power event was to be held across town in Roxbury in the Reggie Lewis Track and Athletic Center. Before we set out, we read from the

Qur'an. The *surah* for the Night of Power speaks of this night as a night when time meets the timeless and angels draw near the earth. It is a night "better than a thousand months." I have always thought the night has something in common with Christmas Eve, when the Word of God comes close to us, for the Qur'an and Christ as divine Word are surely the analogous elements of the Muslim and Christian traditions.

We all bundled up in our parkas and set out in the minivan for Roxbury. Along with hundreds of others we walked into the impressive new Reggie Lewis Track and Athletic Center, passing glass-windowed exercise rooms, track and training rooms, and all the athletic glitz of American sports. The prayer room for the night was a huge triple gymnasium with basketball hoops everywhere. We stacked our shoes at the edge of the gym and lined up on the blue tarps to pray with nearly a thousand Muslims. Our two boys, Sokol and Kreshnik, joined the men. We knelt in the back with the girls, all of us at an angle, facing one corner of the gym toward the *qibla,* the direction of Mecca. We chatted a bit with our neighbors, an Ethiopian woman to my left and two African-American women in front of us. The Ethiopian woman spread her parka on the floor in front of me, so my face would not touch the plastic tarp as we prayed. A woman from Ethiopia welcomed me, not as a stranger but as another worshiper, to a place in the city where I have lived for thirty years.

When I first began visiting mosques in the course of my research, I was not at all certain about prayer. It was more appropriate for me as a researcher to sit in the rear of the congregation, respectfully present but not a participant. As a Christian I felt comfortable praying in my own way but not in the midst of the Muslim community. That night, however, there was no question. In the presence of these young people I asked not only the inner question, "What does it mean for me to pray in the midst of this community?" but rather, "What would it mean for me *not* to pray here in the midst of this community?" The prayers began. "Allahu Akbar!" proclaimed the Imam. "God is Greater!" I bowed, knelt, and could not but agree. God is greater than we as Christians and Muslims can know or imagine.

How do I think about the one I call God, listening to the beautiful, haunting recitations of the Qur'an in Arabic, a Methodist in a sea of Muslims, bowing in prayer with people who both are and are not my spiritual family and kin? During Ramadan I had been reading a book of Seyyed Hossein Nasr, *A Young Muslim's Guide to the Modern World*, hoping that at some point these young Muslims would turn to it as well. In the chapter on God, he writes:

> The Islamic doctrine of God emphasizes beyond everything and above everything His Oneness. "Say *Allah* is One" (CXII:1), the One who "neither begets nor is begotten" (CXII:3), Who cannot be brought into any relation that would in one way or another eclipse His Absoluteness, the One who has no like . . . and the One Who is indivisible. This oneness of God, which is emphasized so much in the Noble Qur'an, refers to God's Essence, His Dhat. However, *Allah* also has Names and Qualities.[8]

The many names of God display these qualities: the Compassionate, the Source of Mercy, the Forgiver, the Sustainer, the Knower, the Hearer, the Seer. Nasr continues, "These Names which the Qur'an calls the Beautiful Names of *Allah*, are the means whereby *Allah* reveals himself to mankind."[9] God is not only transcendent but is also close to us, as the Qur'an puts it, "nearer than the jugular vein." God is at the center of our very being, and the heart of the believer, so Muslims say, is the throne of the Compassionate God. If we glimpse God in this way, there is no reason we cannot stand together, all of us, in prayer.

The Sri Lakshmi Temple

My third stop in this January journey was the next Saturday morning. It was cold and blustery as I drove out the Massachusetts Turnpike to Ashland, the Boston suburb where ten years ago the Hindu community of New England built their first temple up from the ground, the Sri Lakshmi Temple. I came to know people in this community in 1990 as they prepared for the temple dedication. They had poured their energy, time, and love into the creation of this place in a fashion that was completely familiar to me from my own participation as a church member in the finance and building committees or in volunteer painting days. My Hindu friends had the divine images of Vishnu, Ganesha, and Lakshmi crafted of granite in India. The images were still in their packing crates when first I saw them. The ceremonies of dedication to which I was invited included a week of rites by which these images were consecrated and enlivened with the living presence, the breath, of the divine.

Hindus speak of Brahman in the most ultimate of terms, terms even Tillich would have found challenging. Brahman is that reality across which space and time, past, present, and future are woven, warp and weft.[10] Brahman does not lend itself to positive description, but can be described only by negation—not this, not this, not this.[11] Words and speech are inadequate to describe this one. Yet from another perspective, we can also speak of Brahman by infinite affirmation—it is this, it is this, it is this. It is the beyond that is also within. A story from the Chandogya Upanishad makes the point:

> "Bring me a fig," said the teacher.
> "Here it is," said the student.
> "Break it open, what do you see there?"
> "These very little seeds," said the student.
> "Break one of those little seeds open, what do you see there?"
> "Nothing at all, sir," said the student.
> "From that which you do not see, which seems to be nothing at all, this great fig tree grows. That is the Real, Brahman. That is the soul within, atman. That art thou."[12]

This reality is one, whether we stretch our imaginations to the furthest limit of the infinite, or look within toward the deepest ground of being.

At Sri Lakshmi temple the community boldly and with no sense of contradiction invited that infinite reality that has no limit of shape or form to be present in this shape and form, an image of granite. It is called an *archa avatara,* literally an "image incarnation." When the temple was dedicated and the images installed in 1990, I watched with fascinated amazement a cycle of rites I had never seen in my years in India: the *prana-pratishtha* rites through which breath is established in the image and the ritual "eye opening" through which the pupils are carved on the face of the image, so that the worshipers can hold the divine presence in their gaze. The beholding of God's image is called *darshan,* literally "seeing." It means more than seeing with the eyes, however. *Darshan* means using ours eyes to encounter the powerful and beautiful gaze of God. The granite image is not in the Hindu view an "idol" of mere stone but a lens rather, through which we direct our human sight toward the divine.

Now, nearly ten years later, I went to the temple with some students on that Saturday morning in January to attend the *abhisheka,* the weekly service honoring Lord Vishnu with a royal shower. My friend Priya was there, a woman about my age. She is a microelectronic engineer who works on space technology during the week and a devout Hindu who is active in temple life on the weekends. I stood just behind her outside the inner sanctum as the priest chanted in Sanskrit the "Vishnu Sahasranama," the Thousand Names of Vishnu, while he made a series of honor offerings to the eight-foot-high image. He poured water over the head and body of the image, then milk, water, honey, yogurt, turmeric, orange juice, and aromatic sandalwood paste. There was a final oblation of water and then the curtain was closed.

When we saw Vishnu again he was clothed in silk, and the priest presented offerings of fruit, water, and incense and finally the oil lamps of *arati.* All our senses were alert to the presence of the divine. Gracefully moving the oil lamp with its many wicks before the face of Vishnu, the priest illumined each feature of the divine face. Turning from his offerings to Vishnu, he came out of the inner sanctum and presented the oil lamp to each of us. Priya passed her fingertips through the flame and touched the blessings to her eyes and forehead, and so did I. The priest distributed the water scented with camphor that had bathed the image, spooning a drop of it into our hands to sip. Again, as with my prayers on the Night of Power, I asked myself, "What does it mean to me, as a Christian, to sip water that has bathed the image of Lord Vishnu?" And again, I found myself wondering, "What would it mean *not* to?"

To Priya and my Hindu friends at the temple, the one they call God with a thousand names stretches across space and time, past, present, and future, and graciously comes into being in name and form and in ways that often surprise us. The image incarnation is one of the ways through which the divine graciously becomes present, so that we may worship and practice the arts of relationship: love, devotion, reciprocity, and hospitality. The Vaishnava Hindus have a profound and complex theology of Vishnu. They speak of God in two dimensions as the one who is wholly transcendent and as simultaneously accessible. God's accessibility to us as human beings is the manifestation of grace alone. God graciously becomes present in name and form, in temple and image, so that we may apprehend the divine and glimpse the divine glory. God's presence here in the world is limited not by God's capacity to be present but only by our capacity to see, to sense, and to be alert to the many forms of that presence. Not to sip the water that had washed Vishnu's form would for me indicate that I did not think God could be fully present in this sanctum on that Saturday morning. But I did think God was present and I sipped gratefully.

My teacher and colleague, John Carman, wrote on one of the great Vaishnava theologians, Ramanuja, who introduces his 11th-century commentary on the Bhagavad Gita with a synopsis of this Vaishnava theology. Ramanuja begins by describing the ultimacy of Vishnu who is "an ocean of auspicious attributes of matchless excellence inherent in his nature . . . knowledge, untiring strength, sovereignty, immutability, creative power, and splendor." Vishnu is

unchanging, immortal, and "cannot be grasped by speech and thought."
Even so, as Ramanuja puts it, this same immortal one is simultaneously a "shoreless ocean of compassion, gracious condescension, for-
giving love [or motherly affection (vatsalya)], and generosity." Thus
the immortal one assumes bodily form over and over, overwhelmed
as he is by love for human beings.[13] Thus Vishnu has come to reside
in Ashland, Massachusetts.

Thinking about God in the midst of multiple monotheisms

None of these three traditions has a simple theology. Each affirms
the supremacy of a God who cannot be fully known or named, and
each affirms the reality of many names. Each tradition is monotheistic, and yet Christianity, Islam, and Hinduism are monotheistic in
very different ways. The more closely we look, we realize that there
are many monotheisms. How do we think of God, then, in the midst
of these multiple monotheisms? How do we think of God in the
universe of many faiths? On a personal level, how do I think of God
as I make this experiential translation from Christian to Muslim to
Hindu communities?

These are not just theoretical questions of interest only to the likes
of me, since I am a student of Hindu religious traditions and cultures,
have lived in India, and have visited more Hindu temples perhaps than
any living Methodist. I cannot avoid these questions, because they follow me around through my work, my life, and my worship. Versions
of these questions arise for each of us, at least if we take the trouble
to begin to know our neighbors of other faiths. I want, therefore, to
pass these questions on to you so that you may carry them with you as
you come to know the faith of Jews, Muslims, Hindus, Buddhists, or
Sikhs. They are questions that are increasingly important in all the
many places where interreligious dialogue is on the agenda. This
includes not only big cities like Los Angeles and Washington, D.C.,
which have old and well-established interfaith councils, but also cities
like Lincoln, Nebraska, and Columbia, South Carolina, where visionary citizens have boldly initiated experiments and partnerships in

interfaith dialogue. The question of how we, as people of faith, situate ourselves in relation to other families of faith is not only ours as Christians but also ours as Jews, Muslims, Hindus, and Buddhists. All of us live in the new world in which the proximity and intermingling of people of many faiths is a fact of our global life and increasingly our local lives as well.

A religiously diverse society

As the 21st century begins, our neighbors here in the United States are of many religious traditions. The post-1965 immigration has made American society religiously diverse as never before. Los Angeles and Chicago are cities with a complex Buddhist life found nowhere in Asia. At least as many Muslims as Jews live in the United States. Huge Hindu temples have risen in the suburbs of Atlanta, Nashville, Louisville, and Houston. We have Hindu colleagues at work and Hindu surgeons in our hospitals. I have a multitude of Hindu, Muslim, and Buddhist students in my classroom. The Pluralism Project, which I direct at Harvard University, has tried over the past decade to map the changing religious landscape across America.[14]

Not only has our religious architecture begun to change, our civic and public institutions have begun to change as well. Muslims take time for prayer in the workplace at the Whirlpool Corporation in Nashville or at an executive office building in New York. In 1998 the new Denver airport created a shelter where Muslim cabbies may pray one of the required five-times-daily prayers while they are on duty. During the month of Ramadan in 1999, American Muslims broke the Ramadan fast in the State Department at the end of a day of fasting. Secretary of State Madeleine Albright greeted the Muslim community on that occasion. In 1998 the Night of Power was observed at the United States Pentagon, and Deputy Secretary of Defense Dr. John J. Hamre was asked to speak. He began by expressing the "tremendous honor" this was for him. "I am a Lutheran in my own religious background and not a Muslim," he said, "so I cannot fully appreciate how important this Night of Power is for all of you. But I can understand why this Night of Power is deeply important to you, because I am a religious person myself."[15]

Our newfound proximity as neighbors has given us not only new civic questions that we work on as citizens, but also new theological questions with which we wrestle as people of faith. Theological questions, however, are not simply theoretical or important only to theologians and to those of us who are here. They are for all of us because they have to do with how we think about God, who is the dimension of depth that roots and grounds our lives and the one "in whom we live and move and have our being." They have to do with how we think of ourselves when we are alone in the silence of our hearts. They have to do with how we think of our own religious communities in these new times and how we think of our neighbors of other faiths, not just neighbors around the world, but neighbors across the street.

Is God Listening or Not?

These questions are not ours alone as Christians. People like ourselves—Hindu, Buddhist, Muslim, Jewish, and Sikh—are also asking them. In his novel, *The Book of Lights*, Chaim Potok tells of a rabbi from New York who is traveling in Japan during the Korean War on one of his periods of leave. He visits what is likely a Buddhist temple with a friend named John. He saw a man standing before an image of a Buddha or *bodhisattva*, his eyes closed, deeply absorbed in what he would call prayer. The rabbi turned to his friend and asked:

> "Do you think our God is listening to him, John?"
> "I don't know, chappy. I never thought of it."
> "Neither did I until now. If he's not listening, why not? If he is listening, then—well, what are we all about, John?"[16]

The implications of this brief exchange are clear enough and deeply theological. If God is not listening, what kind of God would that be? Could it be the God who created heaven and earth and all that is within it? Could it be the "Fountain ever flowing, Without whom nothing is, All perfect gifts bestowing?" But if God is listening, then what are we all about, who have claimed such a special relationship with God?[17] This is not a question about God's listening at all but a question about our own conception of "our God" vis-à-vis the faith of others. Is our God listening in the Saturday morning recitation of the Thousand Names of Vishnu? Is our God listening to the communal prayers of a thousand Muslims on the Holy Night when angels draw near the earth? This is the central question. There are different ways we may answer this, and I will offer a response as a Christian.

One response: No, God is not listening

The first response would be to say, "No, God is not listening. This Vishnu, honored by Hindu friends on a Saturday morning, is not God. Indeed, this granite form of Vishnu is a graven image, an idol." I know Christians who would stand by this response, saying, "Our God does not listen to the prayers of Hindus or Muslims. They are offered in vain." In the fall of 1999 the Southern Baptist Convention published a prayer guide to enable Christians to pray for Hindus during their fall festival of lights, called Diwali. It spoke of the 900 million Hindus who are "lost in the hopeless darkness of Hinduism . . . who worship gods which are not God."[18] There are Christians who seem to have no trouble at all speaking of "our God" in exclusivist terms.

The problem with such a response, however, is that it misunderstands both the image of Vishnu and the faith of the Hindu. Those who worship him speak of Vishnu as the supreme God, creator and sustainer, who strides through the universe, measuring its length, breadth, and height. It is an image as old as the Hebrew Bible. Hindus do not see Vishnu's image as a "graven image" but as a consecrated image. It is not a piece of stone where one's vision stops but a lens through which one's vision is directed toward the divine. Precisely this way of understanding the divine image would enable Priya to understand the bread and the wine of the Eucharist, should she come with me to church. This is not an act of cannibalism, as any outsider might easily imagine from the words of the Christian sacrament, but an act of the deepest symbolism.

The American Hindus who carried placards protesting the Southern
Baptist prayer guide before Second Baptist Church in Houston did so
not because they were averse to being the focus of Christian prayers,
but because the characterization of their religious tradition was so ill-
informed and ignorant. As I would put it in the language of my own
tradition, it is fine for Baptists to witness to their faith; indeed it is
incumbent upon us all Christians to do so. But it is not fine for us to
bear false witness against neighbors of other faiths.

A second response: Yes, God is listening, but . . .

A second response might be this: God is listening, but it is "our God"
who does the listening. As C. S. Lewis once put it, "I think that every
prayer which is sincerely made even to a false god . . . is accepted by
the true God, and Christ saves many who think they do not know
him."[19] In this view the God whom we know through the language
and faith of our Christian tradition encompasses all this. This image
of Vishnu, whatever it means to Hindus, is a glimpse of that same
God, a ray of that same light, the fullness of which we know in the
complex unity of Father, Christ, and Spirit. This God to whom our
Muslim brothers and sisters bow is revealed, though only in part, in
the Qur'an but fully in the Word of God, Jesus Christ.

    Yet there is a problem here, too: How do we know? What is it in
our tradition that gives us the confidence to say we alone know the
fullness of God? Where did our religious humility go? Can we really
say that we know God completely even from what we know of God
in Christ and from our experience of the Holy Spirit? Can we really
affirm that "our God" is God in God's fullness? This "inclusivist" view
presumes that everything we encounter in the world of faith can be
included under the great, wide tent of our own tradition.

A third response: There is no such God as "our God"

Let me pose a third response, one that brings me closer to theological honesty and to my own experience: There is no such God as "our

God." In this view God is not ours; on the contrary, we are God's. We presuppose now that we may actually learn something new about God, if we attend carefully to the faith of the Vaishnava Hindu, just as they might learn something new about the one they call Vishnu if they attend to ours. We might come to a wider and deeper relationship with God by attending to the prayers of Muslims, and Muslims might be free of some of the simple stereotypes of Christians by attending more carefully to our own Christian language. No simple equations apply here, for God is larger than our understandings.

Most of us who are Christian speak of God as Trinity, but not because the trinitarian understanding of God is set forth in the Bible. The trinitarian view of God is rather a way of addressing the complexity of our experience of God. We speak of God as creator. We speak of God who is not only "in the beginning" but also in our midst today as the Christ, who accompanies us through life and into death. And we speak of God who is Spirit—the flame, the breath, the bird, and the dynamic presence of God-in-motion right here. We speak of God in this way not because there are three different gods, but because there are three interrelated ways of encountering and apprehending the living God. So it is with Vishnu. Here too we find a complex language, a language of supremacy and accessibility, of glory and grace. The image of Vishnu does not invite us to judge, for who are we to judge? It rather invites us to find out more about Vishnu as creator, Vishnu as the one who comes into being in age after age, Vishnu as the one who is with us in the temple and in the home shrine in the kitchen cupboard.

If none of us owns the universe of faith, then honest inquiry enriches us all. The term "theism" is used to describe the ways in which we imagine, understand, speak of, and experience our interrelation with "God." Theism means the human understanding of God. It is clear, even from my brief January journeys, that there are many theisms. There are even many monotheisms, that is, many ways of understanding God as one. We who are Christian are monotheists in quite a different key from the monotheism of our Jewish and

Muslim neighbors. When Hindus speak of the one across whom space and time are woven, warp and weft, known in a multitude of forms and in no form, they articulate a profound and very different monotheism.

Some theologians today say we should move beyond theism, but I am not ready for that move. I, for one, am nourished and enlivened by the God-language in which I live. I feel a sense of living relatedness to God as source and fountain of life, God as companion in the brother I call Jesus, God as living, mothering, flaming spirit. I will not relinquish the richness of these images and these realities. But I am convinced that it is time for us to understand all our theisms as aspects of a global multitheism. By this term I do not mean the multitude of heavenly beings implied by the word polytheism. I speak rather of a theism that recognizes openly and explicitly what is simply a fact. There is a multitude of theisms, many understandings of God, even within the same religious tradition. In this context each of us recognizes that any understanding of God cannot be complete. Many theistic languages speak of God. When we recognize how profoundly this is so and how profoundly multitheistic we human beings are, we will be able to move from *competitive theism* and the religious and political strife it has produced to a *dialogical theism* in which we both learn from and challenge one another in our understandings of God.

Standing on holy ground

On my own path over the past three decades I have stopped a thousand times to take off my shoes. Often when I do stop, I think of the voice that spoke to Moses from the burning bush: "Remove the sandals from your feet, for the place on which you are standing is holy ground." (Exod. 3:5)

I kick off my sandals at the door of a tiny temple on the riverfront in Banaras, at the door of the huge Padmanabhaswami temple in Trivandrum, and the door of the sanctum of Srisailam in the hills of Andhra Pradesh.

I unlace my hiking books at the temple of Siva at Kedarnath, fourteen thousand feet above sea level, and stand with pilgrims who have made the whole trip barefoot.

I add my shoes to a mountain of Reeboks and Nikes at the door of the new Durga Mandir in Fairfax, Virginia.

I take off my shoes at the entry to the Ganesha Temple in Nashville.

I take off my shoes and place them in the orderly shoe racks in the entryway of the Sikh gurdwara in Fremont, California.

I take off my shoes in the little vestibule of the Jain Temple in Norwood where I have come for their annual Festival of Forgiveness.

I take off my shoes at the entry to the prayer room of a huge mosque made from a converted movie theatre in downtown Chicago.

I take off my shoes on the porch of a new Thai Buddhist temple set against a background of Douglas fir in Auburn, Washington.

And that cold Saturday morning in January I put my shoes in the shoe racks by the door of the Sri Lakshmi Temple in Ashland, and pile my shoes with those of our Kosovar teens at the edge of the gymnasium in Roxbury.

When we take off our shoes, we stand before God having relinquished any human claim to the earth beneath our feet. Shoes are the simplest of our possessions, and when we stand shoeless, we are wholly human before God, whether we are Christian or Sikh, Muslim or Hindu. Not that all these places are holy, but something happens there, in the presence of which I should stand attentive, quiet, and barefoot in reverence. That something is a relationship with the divine, the one we call God.

More than sixty years ago at the International Missionary Council in Tambaram, South India, a missionary and teacher, A. G. Hogg, who had lived many years in India, rose to his feet and asked rhetorically:

> Is there any such thing as a religious faith which in quality and texture is definitely not Christian, but in the approach to which one ought to put the shoes off the feet, recognizing that one is on the

holy ground of a two-sided commerce between God and man? In nonChristian faith may we meet with something that is not merely a seeking, but in real measure a finding, and a finding by contact with which a Christian may be helped to make fresh discoveries of his [or her] own finding of God in Christ?

Like this mission educator more than half a century ago, I am certain there is. In the approach to another's faith I have often been moved to take off my shoes, for the ground I have approached is holy ground. It is holy not only because of its sanctity for Hindus, Buddhists, or Muslims, but also because just there God might surprise us and challenge us to a deeper and stronger faith.

Follow-up Questions

M   How would a pastor who wants to engage people in this dialogical theism do so? It is easy to gather them. But what topic do you select? Where do you begin?

DE The first place to start is with inquiry. The biblical injunction is clear: Meet your neighbors. In almost any part of this country you can find neighbors of other faiths. Since the 1965 Immigration Act people from all over the world have come here with their distinctive faiths and traditions. Our encounter with these neighbors begins not so much with a set of ideas as with learning to know them as people.

Q   Would it do any good if in our public schools we had classes in comparative religion, so that the children would understand at an early age what the different religions are?

DE That is the nub of it. Teaching about religion is not a constitutional question for courts to decide. It is important for many reasons. Move beyond our relative religious illiteracy. Religion is part of history, social studies, and literature. We produced the CD-ROM *On Common Ground: World Religions in America* for just that reason, to help school teachers. It brings the voices of other religions into the classroom. It is important to hear what Muslims have to say about prayer or whether women should or should not wear head scarves.

Q   I am a natural scientist. As I study world religions, I find that they are all reformations of an earlier religion that helped these people to better adapt to their environment. Does that help us to understand the development of religions?

DE It would be interesting to explore that. I myself am not so much interested in how religions came about. I do not think we understand a religion best by understanding its origins. Part of what we face today is the need to appropriate and understand the ongoing life of these traditions. Each has taken on a distinctive dynamic. In regard to the Bible, for example, it is important to know not only what went into its creation but also what we make of it today.

Q I was a naval officer and in my travels came to know many of the religious traditions about which you have been speaking. As a teacher I have found it helpful to use the concept of the *logos*— "in the beginning was the Word," and so on—in seeking to understand them. Please comment.

DE As a Christian I also find that concept helpful, especially because the idea of speaking of Christ as the Word—the one who was in the beginning with God, and without whom not one thing came into being—that idea helps us seek that *logos* throughout all creation. It also helps us to set in context some of the exclusivist passages that we find, for example, in the Gospel according to St. John. Think of John 14:6, "I am the way, and the truth, and the life. No one comes to the Father except through me." Some Christian people take that one verse as a dogma rather than as a response of Jesus to his anxious disciples on the night before he died. For Christians such as these that verse has become the key in thinking about how to deal with other faiths. But the task in interpreting the text is to ask, "Who is this 'I' of 'I am the way'?" It is the "I" of the *logos* in the Gospel of John.

Q Comment, please, on the missionary efforts of the Christian churches, including your own. In many ways it appears to me a kind of cultural arrogance.

DE It does and does not. When you look at the tremendous diversity of Christianity around the world today—the sheer energy of Latin American, African, or Asian Christianity, for example—you have to say that something good grew from the missionary response to the command of Jesus to go into all the world. But mission also traveled in the company of empire. That gave Christianity in many parts of the world a bad name. The issue today is how to construe the desire of Christians to share their faith and witness to it in a context of mutuality. Mission then becomes a mutual witness, not a monologue about what we have learned. Our willingness to inquire into and hear from others about what they also have learned is part of the dialogue involved in mission today. I need to add that we will have to do some trust building, because there are many who do not trust us.

Q Will we ever find a common ground to pray genuinely with one another in view of these multiple theisms? Or at best will we be able only to pray for one another?

DE It is hard to know. We are so much at the beginning of this effort. Part of the question is whether we can pray in the company of one another. We can usually pray deeply and sincerely in our own way and in our own language. When I stand in the Hindu temple that is the question I ask myself. I do not pray in the same way as my friend Priya. It is not important that we be of one accord in thinking about what goes on in both our hearts. But there are opportunities for real prayer where we pray in the company of one another, where we listen in to one another. Occasionally we will find language in which we can pray together. Some would say that the group that gathers for prayer is our most intimate family. It is not, therefore, something that we may want to share with other people. But I think we are at the beginning of a time when we can share that intimate language.

Q What do you think of those of us whose personal beliefs encompass pieces of different faiths? I was raised a Catholic but I am also a student of *A Course of Miracles*. I also believe in the strong possibility of reincarnation. Can these beliefs be reconciled?

DE This is a good example of what I mean by saying that faith is not abstract but comes together in the person. We all hear negative reactions to the syncretism of "shopping cart" religion. But I understand it. The Christian faith itself would be something very different if we had not borrowed (and stolen!) all the way through our history, including some pagan practices. If we can bring them together in some pattern of faith, that is good. The real challenge is to find some community of people where we can be ourselves in this faith.

Q In my family I have an older brother who is a Hare Krishna, a sister who is a Muslim, a younger brother who is a fundamentalist and a sister whose son converted to Judaism. [*Laughter*] When we got together for my father's seventieth birthday there were lots of religious divisions at the first. Yet we could come to a unity of heart in honoring God in our relationship with one another. There's something in e. e. cummings about how the one who pays attention to the syntax of things will never kiss you. When we stopped paying attention to the syntax of things, we encountered God in one another. How do we translate the encounter with God into a broader human family?

DE Your family is a good example of how you do it! The issue is one of relationships. What after all has primacy? It is the glue of these family relationships that holds you together. This is the kind of experience that you can find all over this country: people coming together intentionally as a community across the lines of religious division to seek some common language, and to find also where they differ. Our differences are as important as our commonalities. It is not a question of trying to find the lowest common denominator. That will not satisfy. It is more a question of encountering our differences richly and deeply.

Q Last New Year's I was in the old city of Jerusalem and watched with wonder as Christians, Muslims, and Jews went to their services. I found a tolerance there, but it was a cold tolerance. Is cold tolerance our future? Idealistically what could our future be?

DE I am a modest fan of tolerance. It beats hate crimes. But tolerance does not require that we know anything about one another. We cannot live in a world with only an ethic of tolerance. We need an ethic of dialogue and encounter that will let us come to know the people whom otherwise we would just tolerate.

In Fremont, California, a United Methodist church and a mosque have bought property together and built side by side on a street they call "Peace Terrace." The church is pretty humble, the mosque tremendous. The question is, what will that proximity of living together on the same street mean? Will it be cold tolerance or real dialogue? That is the question.

Q Are there any ideas of God that you would say are inauthentic? Would you be willing to take off your shoes at a church of Scientology or of Jehovah's Witnesses, for instance?

DE I won't name names but we don't hang up our minds when we take off our shoes! The critical thing in the encounter with other religions is not just warm-hearted hand-holding. (That is true also within our religious traditions.) True dialogue is a challenging thing. I would refuse to enter into dialogue with almost no one, but there are many places where I would not take off my shoes. And there are places where I would take them off and wish I hadn't. [*Laughter*] I don't know if we can decide in advance. At the very least we want people to define themselves and not be predefined by our ideas of them. We know—or assume we know—who the "Jews" or the "Muslims" or the "Catholics" are and sometimes make misjudgments. It is important to let people speak for themselves, and dialogue is the first step.

3

An Ocean of God:
The Interconnectedness of All Being
Rabbi Lawrence Kushner

Lawrence Kushner is a rabbi, author of ten books, lecturer, scholar of Jewish mysticism, storyteller, and a leader of personal and institutional spiritual renewal within Judaism.

His books include: *Eyes Remade for Wonder; Invisible Lines of Connection: Sacred Stories of the Ordinary; The Book of Miracles; The Book of Words: Talking Spiritual Life, Living Spiritual Talk; God Was in This Place and I, I Did Not Know: Finding Self, Spirituality and Ultimate Meaning; The River of Light: Spirituality, Judaism, and the Evolution of Consciousness; Honey from the Rock: An Easy Introduction to Jewish Mysticism;* and *The Book of Letters: A Mystical Hebrew Alphabet.*

He has been the rabbi of Congregation Beth El in Sudbury, Massachusetts, for twenty-eight years. He originated the concept of synagogue family fellowship groups; led his congregants to publish their own prayerbook (*Purify Our Hearts*), the first gender-neutral liturgy in the Jewish tradition; and has conducted over seventy-five *kalla* weekends for personal religious growth. He was the first Rabbinic Chairman of Reform Judaism's Commission on Religious Living.

A native of Detroit, Michigan, he graduated Phi Beta Kappa from the University of Cincinnati and was ordained a rabbi from Hebrew Union College in 1969. For over a decade, he has been on the faculty of the Hebrew Union College–Jewish Institute of Religion in New York, and is a regular commentator on NPR's *All Things Considered.*

When Professor Borg first invited me to participate in this conference, I was, of course, honored. But I was also a little puzzled. I thought, at first, "God at 2000," the man is inviting me to some kind of e-mail address! You know, God @ 2000 *dot* com, or *dot* org; no, *dot* net. Yes, that's it: God at 2000 *dot* net. This got me to wondering that if God *did* have a Web site, what would it look like? I mean, how would you get there? And if you could get there, how many links would you find? And once you did, where could you go? Just imagine: the server to end all servers. Operating at speeds faster than broadband. Instantaneous connections with everyone and everything. No waiting. Remember: Time is just God's way of making sure everything doesn't happen all at once.

That's the whole idea of the Net isn't it? Human beings, driven by the lure of money and power, invent a way to connect everyone and everything. But, of course and alas, the old Kabbalistic myths have *already* beaten us to the punch. Everything is already joined to everyone and everything else. This web of meaning is so complete, so perfect that it has no discernable parts at all. It has no beginning, no end. It has no boundaries. It is the substrate of all being, the font of creation. Everything that exists comes from it, just as everything (and everyone), sooner or later, returns to it. But I'm getting ahead of myself.

This thing has three main parts: The first is called Virtual Reality, the second The Ocean of Nothing, and the last Reverence.

Virtual Reality

It was almost ten years ago that one of my sons brought home what was then a new and sophisticated computer game. "It's called 'virtual reality,' Dad," he explained. "You play it by *entering* it. You must imagine that you are actually inside it. You ask yourself, 'What would I do if I really lived in this world?' "

The game was called Myst. (They've since come out with a sequel called Riven.) You pop in the CD, look at the screen, and find yourself on an island. There's a dock, a forest, buildings, stairways. The graphics and sound effects are impressive and convincing. There is no manual, no instructions, no rules. You "go" places by aiming a little pointing finger and clicking. You can look up and down, turn around, climb stairs, wander all around the place. Wherever your curiosity leads you, there are things to discover and remember. There are machines you can operate, a library full of books you can actually open and read. Devotees say the game is properly played over weeks and months. (It's been almost a decade and I *still* haven't finished.)

And the purpose of it all? Why, of course: to figure out what you're doing there. But to do that, you must first figure out how the place works.

What fascinates me here is not yet another sophisticated and clever way to waste time in front of the computer screen. (I can do that with Solitaire and FreeCell.) It is the concept of a game whose purpose is for the player to discover the purpose. Virtual reality, schmirtual reality, this ain't no game. What's going on here? Why am I here? What are the rules?

Upon hearing about all this, a friend who is a professor of English suggested that it seemed a lot like childhood. I'd go further. It may be a lot like adulthood, too. We all find ourselves in "this world" and the "object" seems to be to figure out what we're doing here. Unfortunately, the way most things are connected to one another is not immediately apparent.

After all, meaning is a matter of connections. If something is connected to absolutely nothing—symbolically, linguistically, physically, psychologically—it is literally meaning*less*. And, if something is connected to everyone and everything, it would be supremely meaning*ful*. I suppose it would be God: The One through whom everything is connected to everything else, the Source of all meaning. Religious traditions are the collected "rules of the game." They presume to tell us how the world works. And if you "play by them," you are rewarded (hopefully before it is time to leave) with an understanding of why you are here—with what is otherwise known as the meaning of life.

So, what if there were a virtual reality computer game that was programmed to approximate real life? What would be "the object"? The way I see it, there are only five rules.

The first rule of the game of life is that you cannot decide when to begin playing. One day, out of the blue, you realize it: "Uh-oh, I'm playing the game!" Someone else determined when your game would begin. And it wasn't your parents. They may have known about the birds and the bees and even set out to conceive a child, but they didn't have a clue it was going to be you. And now that they've had a chance to meet you, while they most likely love you, they'd probably have picked somebody else. In religious language, this means that you are a creature. Someone else made you. And you are neither its partner nor its puppet: You are its manifestation, its agent, its child.

The second rule is that you cannot decide when to stop playing the game, either. One day, out of the blue: You're dead. For a slogan on the box of the game of "Life," we could use something I saw on a T-shirt: "Life: You're not going to make it out alive!" That means there's no way you can "win" the game by staying in it forever. No matter how many points, toys, honors, conquests, dollars you accumulate (or books you write), sooner than anyone expects or wants, the game is abruptly over. You hear a little buzzer, the keyboard freezes, the screen goes blank. The game ends without warning. But there's good news: Dying does not mean you lose. It's what you do before you die that determines whether or not you win when you die.

The third rule—just to keep you on your toes—is that each player is issued apparently random, undeserved gifts and handicaps throughout the progress of the game. Figuring out why you got the combination package you did transforms all disabilities into gifts, just as refusing to figure out why you were issued what you received transforms all gifts into disabilities. My father used to say that all men are not created equal. Some get dealt a full house, others a pair of twos. The question therefore is not whether you deserve the hand you were dealt, but how you choose to play it.

The fourth rule is that points are awarded whenever you can discern the presence of the Creator, and then act so as to help others see it, too. The presence of the Creator is not just in objects, but in actions and thoughts and feelings; not just in sunshine and happiness, but in agony, struggle, and death. Remember: Finding the Presence and then acting in such a way as to help others find it, too, is the only way to accumulate game points.

And the last rule is that everything is connected to everything else. And for that reason, "Life" is permeated with meaning. Most of the time we are oblivious to it. We go about our lives as if every event were an accident. And then something happens and we see the connection, the presence of the Creator. For just a moment it is unmistakable. We are astonished that we couldn't see it until now. All creation is one great unity. There are no coincidences.

Throughout all creation, just beneath the surface, joining each person to every other person and to every other thing in a luminous organism of sacred responsibility, we discover invisible lines of connection.

Now that's *my* idea of a game.

No big-time mystic

Don't get me wrong, I'm not what you'd call a big-time mystic. I don't think I've even had a mystical experience. I have never heard a chorus of angels singing, nor have I seen a vision of Ezekiel's chariot. (Once, when I had a high fever, my wife told me that I did say a few things that made no sense, but I've never spoken in tongues either.) Yet of all the religious labels currently available, "mystic" still fits best.

Permit me a working definition: A mystic is someone who has the gnawing suspicion that just beneath the *apparent* contradictions, brokenness, and discord of this everyday world lies a hidden unity. Somehow—even though any fool can see that superficially it makes no sense—everything is connected. It's all one, or, as the Jews say, God is One.

Think about it. What's the alternative? That reality is *only* what you can see and only a few things are mechanically connected? Everything else is just dumb luck, happenstance, chance, playing the lottery, rolls of the dice? Or, if you believe there's a God, that God is only involved in some things but not *every*thing? No, for a mystic, God is not only involved in *everything,* even more, God *is* everything.

Fleeting glimmers of this eternal truth last for only a moment or two and then they're gone. I'm talking about everyday, garden variety epiphanies. No Mormon Tabernacle Choir singing Handel's "Hallelujah Chorus," just "Oh, yes. I had forgotten but now I see it again: Everything is connected."

San Mateo-Hayward Bridge duck

Last Thanksgiving morning, for instance: My old friend Alan and I have left our families for a few hours to go for a walk through a wildlife refuge on the edge of San Francisco Bay. The morning haze is chilly and still. The atmosphere is so dense that, within a few hundred yards, we can no longer see or even hear the traffic from the bridge. We stop our conversation, momentarily distracted by a lone duck silently swimming among the tall grass of the estuary. This duck is moving so slowly it leaves no ripples on the water. For a moment I, too, leave no ripples. I think to myself: There is no past, no future, only this creature, swimming, leaving no wake. Alan and I, the duck, the haze, the cars on the bridge I cannot hear or see: We are all one. Then it's over.

The Ocean of Nothing

Let us begin with two simple Hebrew words. The first word is *yesh.* It means "somethingness" or better, simply "isness." The other word is its opposite: *ayin.* It means, you guessed it, "nothingness"—not zip, but the absence of any "thingness." And, if some "thing" is no "thing," then it has no boundaries. It is literally bound*less.* Therefore *ayin* is also without beginning, without end, another name for eternity.

Jewish mystical tradition invests these two words with cosmic, meta-physical significance. *Yesh* comes to refer to the created world, the one in which we spend most of our time. But *yesh* connotes much more than just the material or physical world. It includes spatial, temporal, intellectual, even emotional reality also. The key idea here is that all the things of *yesh* have definitions, beginnings and ends, and, above all, *boundaries*. Ladies and gentlemen, I give you the world of *yesh* in all its variegated splendor: We buy it, sell it, think it, feel it, insure it, trade it, imagine it, hoard it, and, like people in a flood, we futilely try to grab as much as we can while it floats by, under the illusion that it will make us powerful and save us. Living in the world of *yesh* is not bad—indeed, it's inescapable and often beautiful. It's only dangerous if you think that's all there is.

Ayin, on the other hand, connotes not the absence of being but the absence of any boundaries, that is, no thing, a *nothing* that encompasses and permeates all creation. *Ayin* is therefore the font of all being, the substrate of creation. (The Kabbalists called God *Eyn Sof,* "endless.") Not only can't you own *ayin,* you cannot alter it, change it, or affect it in any way whatsoever. You cannot point to it. You probably can't even accurately say as much about it as I've already said. It is like you're a wave and *ayin* is the ocean. You and I, the watches on our wrists, this building, the trees outside, the people we love, even the love itself, all of creation—they are all the waves, *yesh,* made of that ocean of *ayin,* manifestations of that great underlying nothingness and oneness of all being.[20]

Nothing to see

This reminds me of the time a few years ago when I was reading the mail in my office at the synagogue and one of our fourth-grade teachers came running in.

"Rabbi, we need you right away: They're talking about God!"

I went down to the classroom and began my emergency lesson. "Tell me what you know about God," I asked. A few hands slowly went up.

"God made the world," said one. I wrote "Made the world" on the board.

"God's one," said another. I put it on the board, too.

"God's good," ventured a third. There were a few dissenting votes, but the majority was still for divine beneficence.

Then another child said, "God's invisible." I started to write "invisible" on the board but another kid objected.

"You're wrong. God's visible, He's [sic] right here, right now."

"Oh yeah, I don't see Him. What's He look like?" countered the first.

To which the other said, "That's just it . . . there's nothing to see!"

Drop in the ocean

This reminded me of a teaching we have in the name of Rabbi Yehiel Michal of Zlotchov citing his teacher, Dov Baer of Mezritch in 1777:

> "It's just the opposite of what everyone thinks," he says. "They assume that when they . . . hang on . . . to the things and matters of this world, they amount to something (*yesh*) in their own eyes. They imagine that they are important. But ask yourself: How could anyone who might not wake up the next morning be important? [Such a big shot. Got hit by a truck. Next!] . . . In this way, if you think you are something (*yesh*), then alas, you are nothing (*ayin*). [Don't try this at home!]
>
> If, on the other hand, because of your fusion with the Creator . . . you think of yourself as nothing, then you are very great indeed. You are like the branch of a tree that realizes it's one organic unity with its root. And the root is the One without end—the *Eyn Sof,* the One of Nothing. So, if the branch is one with the root and the root is the One of Nothing, then the branch too ceases to exist as an independent thing; it is no thing."

Michal of Zlotchov concludes, "You become like a single drop of water fallen into the sea. It has returned to its source. It is one with the ocean."[21]

To paraphrase Dov Baer of Mezritch: The work of creation was amazing, for God made something from nothing. But the work of the holy ones is even more extraordinary for they take something and by their actions and intentions transform it back into nothing! If someone asks you what Kushner talked about this afternoon, just tell 'em, "Oh, nothing." Let me conclude these reflections on nothing with a true story.

Reading music

A year ago last fall I turned fifty-five. To increase the likelihood that this milestone would only be a joyous event, my wonderful wife, the bride of my youth, after months of clandestine research, to my utter surprise and dumbfounded astonishment, presented me with a concert-grade, B-flat clarinet. Now this would just be the story of another extravagant and expensive gift were it not for one other fact. Prior to that moment last fall, I had never in my entire life even touched a clarinet! I wasn't even conscious I wanted one.

"How did you know?" I sputtered.

"I just listened," she replied. "For twenty years you've been muttering that someday you'd like to learn how to play the clarinet. I checked with the kids, they heard it, too. Apparently you're the only one who never knew."

Well, I've been taking lessons now for a year and a half. (I come right after an eleven-year-old Asian kid.) I am a little disappointed that I still haven't had any feelers yet from major symphony orchestras, but it's only been sixteen months. And besides, I still can't read music very well. Reading music, it's becoming increasingly clear, will definitely take a few more months.

There are so many nuances: All those little Italian abbreviations, "Every Good Boy Does Fine," dotted eighth notes, keys with six sharps or six flats, funny little squiggles and marks everywhere! And then there's keeping time. To help you count the rhythm, at the end of every measure there is a little vertical bar line. I count: one, two, three, four, end of measure; one, two, three, four, end of measure.

My tutor says, "Why do you pause at the end of each measure?"

I say, "Because there's this little vertical line there."

She says, "You're not supposed to play *that.*"

I say, "I'm not *playing* it."

She says, "Yes, you are. You're pausing at each one!"

I say, "But then how would anyone know it's the end of a measure?"

She sets down her clarinet and turns to face me. (This means she is exasperated and something important is about to come.) "The bar lines are not there. Yes, I know they're written in the sheet music. They're there to make it easier for you to count time but the divisions are only arbitrary superimpositions. They're not *in the music.*"

This reminded me of something I learned from Professor Daniel Matt, currently in the fifth year of a twenty-year-long project of translating the *Zohar.*

We have a word, he once explained, for a leaf, a twig, a branch, a trunk, roots. The words make it easier for us to comprehend reality. But we must be careful not to allow ourselves to fall into the habit of thinking that just because we have words for all the parts of a tree that therefore a tree really has all those parts. The leaf does not know when it stops being a leaf and becomes a twig. Nor does the branch know when it is no longer a branch and now the trunk. And the trunk is not aware that it has stopped being a trunk and is now the roots. Indeed, the roots do not know when they stop being roots and become soil. Nor the soil the moisture, nor the moisture the atmosphere, nor the atmosphere the sunlight. All our names are only arbitrarily superimposed on seamless reality.

The Kabbalists explained it this way. There are two worlds: the *Olam haPrayda,* the world of separation—the one we inhabit most of the time, this world, with its infinite array of discrete and autonomous parts, each with its own name (and, if it's human, with its own agenda)—and then there is the *Olam haYihud,* the world of unity, a radical monism, wherein there are neither parts nor names, where everything is one. Or perhaps more accurately, everything is The One.[22]

It will also come as no surprise that we will predictably understand our relationship with God depending on whichever of the two worlds we happen to inhabit at the moment. Most of the time the world is subdivided into measures, each bordered by vertical bar lines, or parts, each distinguished by its own unique name and geographic coordinates. Our relationship with God here is likewise personal, one of two discrete, autonomous, and independent actors. And as in virtually all classical Western metaphors, God is *other* than the world—creating, designing, supervising, and hopefully running the place.

But the world of separation lies *within* the bosom of the world of unity.[23] Here we have another way to understand how we relate to God. In this world of unity there are no names, no parts, no separations and therefore no relationships. Indeed, strictly speaking, there can't even be a relationship. (What did the Kabbalist say to the hot-dog vendor? Make me one with everything.)

It is all one, The One, The One of All Being, you know, God. In the Yiddish, "*Alles ist Gott!*" And, just as music happens only when we are no longer aware of the discrete notes, measures, rhythms, in the same way. . . meaning comes when we comprehend the unity that is the core of all being, when the world of separation gives way to the world of unity. When, as in the imagination of the Kabbalists, we are finally able to pronounce all of Scripture as one long, uninterruptible Name of God.

But alas, to learn how to make music, you must *first* subdivide the whole score into smaller pieces, each one separated from the other by a little vertical line.

Reverence

This brings us to my third and final observation. It was Tolstoy, I believe, who once observed that the closer you are to an event, the more you think you run it and the further you get from it, the more you realize you don't run anything. This may also be the meaning of the cryptic and tantalizing maxim found in Talmud tractate *Berakhot* 33b, "*Hakol bi-day shamayim, khutz mi-yirat shamayim.* Everything is up to Heaven except whether or not you're reverent." That may just be the only available exercise of freedom: whether or not you will be reverent. If God is the ocean and we are the waves, then it is certainly a serious possibility.

Relax, this doesn't mean that you simply roll over and go with the flow. Indeed, what is set before us often requires seemingly autonomous and courageous action. You are going about your business when you stumble on to something that has your name on it. Or, more accurately, a task with your name on it finds you. Its execution requires inconvenience, self-sacrifice, even risk. Often it comes in the form of another human being. You step forward and encounter your destiny.

Stranger on the bus

A light snow was falling and the streets were crowded with people. It was Munich in Nazi Germany. One of my rabbinic students, Shifra Penzias, told me her great-aunt, Sussie, had been riding a city bus home from work when SS storm troopers suddenly stopped the coach and began examining the identification papers of the passengers. Most were annoyed but a few were terrified. Jews were being told to leave the bus and get into a truck around the corner.

My student's great-aunt watched from her seat in the rear as the soldiers systematically worked their way down the aisle. She began to tremble, tears streaming down her face. When the man next to her noticed that she was crying, he politely asked her why.

"I don't have the papers you have. I am a Jew. They're going to take me."

The man exploded with disgust. He began to curse and scream at her. "You stupid bitch," he roared. "I can't stand being near you!"

The SS men asked what all the yelling was about.

"Damn her," the man shouted angrily. "I'm so fed up. She always does this! My wife has forgotten her papers again!"

The soldiers laughed and moved on.

My student said that her great-aunt never saw the man again. She never even knew his name.

Bosque del Apache

Last story. We read in Exodus 25:20 of the ark of the covenant. It is to be made of acacia wood overlaid with gold and carried by two long poles. And on top of this box containing the tables of the law are to be placed two gold cherubim whose ". . . wings are spread out above, shielding the cover [of the ark] with their wings." These winged angels come up again in Ezekiel 1:24 and 10:14.

The prophet has a psychedelic vision of God on a chariot that's borne by an eagle, a cherub, a lion, and a human being. Each creature had four wings. Ezekiel says: ". . . [It was] like the noise of great waters, I heard the noise of their wings, like the voice of the Almighty. . ."

I am standing in the middle of the New Mexico desert last winter. It is thirty degrees and a half-hour before dawn. We are in the *Bosque del Apache,* the forest of the Apache, a bird sanctuary.

I am not a big-time naturalist but my wife is an avid birder. And so, like spouses do, I tag along.

"For this one," teeth chattering, while sipping coffee from the thermos, I whisper, "I want extra points."

She smiles.

In the distance, the horizon is becoming visible now as a dark ribbon of deep red in the winter chill. And dawn comes. The whole sky explodes into bright orange.

And then, within the next fifteen minutes, we watch in awestruck silence, as 25,000 snow geese, cranes, great blue herons, and God only knows who else, awake from their sleeping on the water and fly off for the next leg of their migration.

They are so close and there are so many of them, I can literally feel the flapping wing-flung wind on my face. The park rangers call it "the flyaway." Last evening they warned: You're never the same after the flyaway. And I understand: Somehow, simply being present to experience this event changes your perception of what it means to be a creature.

And here's the thing that chastens and humbles me: The birds do this all the time. Whether we're here to watch them or not, they land in the waters of the Bosque, and come first light, they fly away into the dawn's early light, a sky full of wings and beaks and feathers on their way to somewhere else. And they do it year after year after year. Just like the great whales do it through the waters of the sea and mitochondria do it through the fluid within our cells. Great flowing streams of life, currents of protoplasm—flying, swimming, running, moving, flowing, praying—doing what they know how to do, doing the only thing they know to do, doing what they were "meant" to be doing, doing what they're "supposed" to do. While I, in my ignorance—obsessed with completing some writing assignment—am doing what I'm supposed to be doing, what I am meant to do. All these creatures, moving on their ways, going about their business, one orchestrated flow of life. My God, I can still feel the wind of their wings on my face.

Probably the holiest ritual moment in ancient Judaism was on the Day of Atonement, Yom Kippur, when the high priest entered the holy of holies in the temple in Jerusalem. He only had one thing to do. He had rehearsed it for months. He had to pronounce one word: the ineffable Name of God. The Name made only of vowel letters. The Name made from the root letters of the Hebrew verb *to be*. A Name that probably initially meant something like, "The One who brings into being all that is." The Name of the One who looks like Nothing.

And the room in which he would speak this Name was so sacred that if, God forbid, he should drop dead of a heart attack once inside, no one else would be able to go back in there to retrieve his corpse!

Rabbi Isaac explained in the *Zohar*[24] that they solved the problem by simply tying a rope around his leg. . . . Rabbi Judah further said that when the priest entered, even *he* closed his eyes—so as not to gaze where it was forbidden to gaze. But, as they sang their praises, he was able to hear the sound of the cherubim's wings. . . .

Liza meets the Shekhina

I thought that was the end of the story until last spring. I was having breakfast at a hotel in Pittsburgh with three other rabbis. We were there for a convention. I don't remember how we got on the topic, but Liza says, "I'll tell you about a time when I felt the wings of the Shekhina." (The *Shekhina* is a Hebrew word for the feminine presence of God. The rabbis often likened her to a bird, landing apparently from out of nowhere, easily frightened. Liza always has neat things to say, but since I had just finished writing about the flapping of wings, I listened carefully.)

"I'm at my obstetrician's for a routine appointment," she says. "This is already my fourth pregnancy, so the doctor and I have been friends for a long time. While she's hooking me up for the ultrasound, we just go on with our conversation. Somehow we had gotten to talking about birth order, and I asked my doctor if her husband was a first child.

" 'Oh no,' she says, 'my husband's a twin.' "

" 'A twin,' I say. 'My God, if I had twins, I'd need a new house, a new husband, a new life!' "

" The obstetrician turns on the ultrasound machine and together we look in reverent silence at the image on the screen."

" 'Here, do you see?' says the doctor, pointing to a tiny line. 'This is the spine.' "

" 'And what's this?' " I ask, pointing to another line on the other side.

"She pauses for a moment. A smile forms on her lips. 'Why, that's the other one. . . .' "

"I could feel the wind of the wings of the *Shekhina* flapping," whispers Liza. "It was as if God had come and gently fluttered open the next page of my life-book. The page had been written there all along. The page was only waiting for me to see it. . . ."

Follow-up Questions

M   Do you realize that you are talking like a contemporary physicist? The new science is full of revelations about the interconnectedness of all being. One of the new words in physics is non-locality. It means there is no such thing as locality, because this atom is related to that and to every other atom.

LK   Why should it surprise us that traditions that are trying to find the truth should every now and then converge?

Q   I've read two of your books. You seemed quite serious there. I didn't know you were quite this humorous.

LK   I believe that theology without humor is blasphemy. [*Laughter*]

Q   How do you as a Jewish rabbi view another rabbi of two thousand years ago, Jesus of Nazareth?

LK   He was a great Jew. [*Laughter*]

Q   Do you view him as a Kabbalist?

LK   Kabbalism did not begin until the thirteenth century. He was good—but not that good. [*Laughter*] My theory is that there is only a finite number of great religious ideas. Sooner or later every religion has them all. [*Laughter*]

Q   I have a question about time. We talk about the space/time continuum. Past, present, and future—are they all one?

LK   Time is a human superimposition on reality. It's our attempt to make sense out of stuff. Don't we say that at moments of extraordinary meaning—not necessarily happy ones—there is a timelessness to those moments? We feel we are above time. We are given permission to see the past and the future in a way that would have been unthinkable just a moment before.

Q In the Jewish tradition there are different understandings of covenant. It seems that the Mosaic covenant is conditional. There is an "if," a necessity of responding in faith in order that the promise be in operation. In the earlier covenants with Noah and Abraham it seems that the promise of relationship is more one way, given in total generosity and independent of our response. Is there a difference?

LK In contemporary Judaism a covenant is a relationship primarily of love, a relationship of mutual expectation. The Torah, so central to Judaism, is a sign of that intimate relationship. It is the way Jews understand their unique relationship with the divine. But it is not exclusive.

Q A Christian, speaking with a rabbi, asked, "Why is it that a Jew always answers a question with another question?" The rabbi replied, "Why not?" That answer ties in with your presentation. If we are going to be in the ocean of nothingness, of which you spoke, then we must continue to search and to question and not to limit the answer.

LK I am a big advocate of questions as opposed to answers. To base a religious philosophy on questions instead of on answers increases the likelihood of wonder and amazement.

When we are talking about the world where everything is all one, one of the things we lose is the ability to have a *relationship* with God because there are no longer parts. Enter that world, and prayer becomes only meditative, simply an awareness. Step back out into the world of separation, and you conjecture about the relationships that exist in many shapes and metaphors.

Q If we are created in God's image, then can we not learn more of God by learning more about our own nature?

LK Absolutely. If we say that God is the ocean and we are the waves, most of what we know about the ocean is a function of what we learn by watching the waves. It's hard to know what is in the depths. All we have is one another. There is a tradition, according to a beautiful Hasidic commentary, that all God gave at Mount Sinai was the first letter of the first word. In Hebrew it is the letter aleph, which has barely a sound. The commentator says that the aleph is two eyes and a nose, meaning every human face. What God revealed at Mount Sinai is that everyone's face is engraved with the content of the revelation and the name of the divine. When we look at one another we realize that we are looking at God.

M The Internet seems to be a fascinating model for you of the interconnectedness of all being.

LK A midrash is a Jewish art form that is not quite commentary and not quite story. It can be understood on the model of the Internet as well. The goal of midrash and of Jewish reading of scripture is to take every word in scripture and turn it blue. That means you can click on any word in scripture and it will take you to another word in scripture. Ultimately, you realize that the whole thing is connected, interwoven and meaningful.

Q On the unity of all things: In my understanding both the Jewish and the Christian traditions place a high priority on the relationship between individuals and God and between individuals and one another. But isn't identity needed for any relationship?

LK We are playing off here the ancient and impossible-to-resolve tension between the two and the one. Most of the time we live in the world of separation, the world of the two. There are two parties; there is a relationship. It is critical that we understand that. But the goal is that the two come together and become one. It is called marriage, or love, or realization, but it will last only for a minute, and then it's back to two again.

Q The story about the ultrasound suggests that you are talking about predestination.

LK If I talk about God being involved in everything and you hear me talk about that from the world of separation, then you are immediately pushed into a theology in which God is the cosmic puppeteer and we are all marionettes, moving jerkily with no free will. I am talking about God as present in all of being. When there are moments of heightened reality and awareness, some-how, even although it makes no rational sense, every sensing human being I have ever talked to says, "Yes, for a moment that's the way it is supposed to be." It is as if we have been given per-mission to stand up on the chair and look out, surveying the whole thing and saying, "Why, of course." But we can stay there only for a moment. Then it's time to make lunch or pay the taxes or do what you've got to do.

Q   In Christian understanding, points are credited to us through the person and work of Jesus Christ. How do you respond to a Christian apologist who would say that religions are superficially the same but fundamentally different?

LK   First, let me share with you an insight into life after death that I gained from a rabbi friend. He says that when you die, they put you in a very comfortable chair and surround you with quadra-phonic sound speakers and a huge video monitor. They begin showing over and over again, very slowly, a movie of everything you ever did in your life. Heaven or hell, you pick! [*Laughter*]

     Imagine that there is an arbitrary finite number of great reli-gious ideas. You have to think about what happens when you die. You need to know how to make atonement. You have got to be aware of the presence of the Creator. Let's say there are fifty-two of these ideas. A deck of cards. All religions are playing with a full deck. The only difference between the religions is the way the deck is stacked. If you are an orthodox Christian the first card is that you are guilty, and that you need help right away. Jews have that card, but it comes up number ten. For Jews, the top card is, What is God wanting me to do now? Orthodox Christians have got that card too, but in a different place.

Q   As we explore this ocean image, where does evil fit in?

LK What is the option? I can say either that God is manifest in all
being, and that there is a bunch of things in creation I don't like,
but God is somehow still in them. That's the end of the book of
Job. God shows Job the ultimate *Wild Kingdom* video—lions rip-
ping apart gazelles, vultures tearing carrion in pieces. God says
to Job: "What do you think of that? I hope you like it, because
I'm in that too. Good-bye." [*Laughter*]

4 God Become Infinitely Larger
Joan D. Chittister, O.S.B.

Joan Chittister is a Benedictine sister, author of twenty books, and a well-known national and international lecturer. She is Executive Director of Benetvision: A Resource and Research Center for Contemporary Spirituality, and past president of the Conference of American Benedictine Prioresses and the Leadership Conference of Women Religious. A theologian, social psychologist, and communication theorist, she has taught on all educational levels.

Among her nineteen books are *Passion for Life: Fragments of the Face of God* and *There Is a Season,* both of which received the First-Place Award from the Catholic Press Association. Her most recent book is *In Search of Belief.* Other books include: *Heart of Flesh: A Feminist Spirituality for Women and Men; Light in the Darkness: New Reflections on the Psalms; Songs of Joy: New Meditations on the Psalms; Beyond Beijing: The Next Step for Women; The Fire in These Ashes: A Spirituality of Contemporary Religious Life; Wisdom Distilled from the Daily;* and *The Rule of Benedict: Insights for the Ages.*

She attended the Fourth United Nations Conference on Women in Beijing as a media representative for the *National Catholic Reporter,* for which she is a regular columnist. She is also an active member of the International Peace Council, an interfaith group of religious and spiritual leaders committed to applying the values of peace, love, and justice to situations of conflict and violence. She has received nine honorary doctorates, and has been recognized by universities and national organizations for her work for justice, peace, and equality for women in the church and society.

Her bachelor's degree in English is from Mercyhurst College, her master's in communication arts is from Notre Dame, and her doctorate in speech communication theory is from Penn State.

She has lectured throughout the United States and Canada, as well as in England, South Africa, Australia, Ireland, Italy, Hungary, the Philippines, New Zealand, and Belgium.

Two seekers inspire a sense of the possibility and potential of this topic, and shape these reflections of mine on "God at 2000."

The first is an old Sufi who was found scratching through the sand in the middle of the road. "What are you doing, Sufi?" pilgrims asked as they passed him, digging and scratching, on their way to the temple.

"I am looking for the treasure I have lost," the old man said. So the pilgrims, good people all, dropped to their knees to help—sifting sand, digging under stones, and sweating under the waxing midday sun. Finally, hungry, soaking wet, and exhausted, one of the travelers said to him at last, "Sufi, are you sure you lost your treasure here?"

And the old man said, "Oh my! No. I didn't lose my treasure here. I lost it over there on the other side of those mountains."

"Well, if you lost it on the other side of the mountains," the people shouted at him, "why, in the name of *Allah*, are you looking for it here?"

The old man said, "I am looking for it here because there is more light here."

My second guide through the complexities of this question is the seeker who asked the holy one: "How are we to seek union with God?"

And the holy one said, "The harder you seek, the more distance you create between God and you."

"Then what does one do about the distance?" the disciple persisted.

And the holy one said, "Understand that it isn't there."

"But does that mean that God and I are one?" the seeker asked.

And the holy one said: "Not one. Not two."

"But how is that possible?" the seeker said. And the holy one said: "The sun and its light, the ocean and the wave, the singer and his song—not one. Not two."[25]

What I have learned about God after a lifetime of seeking is that first, God must be sought in the light, and that second, God does not have to be found.

A Marketplace Full of Ideas about God

If there is anything in the world, however, that may deserve our pity, it may well be the very idea of "God." What else in the history of humankind has been more reviled as fraud, more ridiculed as unprovable or, on the other hand, more glorified out of existence—more condemned to unattainable remoteness—than the notion of God?

A wag wrote once: "First God created us, and then we created God." The insight may be far too true to ignore, and the consequences of it far too distancing to celebrate.

The marketplace is, in fact, full of ideas about God—religious tradition itself not the least of the purveyors of them. Some of these ideas have been helpful to the development of a God-life within me, some of them not.

Whatever the images of God we offer, whatever the effects of them spiritually and socially, I have come to the conclusion over the years that it is precisely our idea of God that is the measure of our spiritual maturity. What we believe about God colors everything we do in the name of God, everything we think about other people, everything we determine about life itself.

And it is not—this consciousness of God—exceptional. No, in the long light of human history, it is not belief in God that sets us apart. Belief in the existence of God may be the very least term of the equation. It is certainly not unique to us, to the West, to Christianity, or even to this sophisticated time in history, the character of which we like to consider so advanced, so "enlightened." In fact, all peoples on earth have come to the juncture where only God is an answer to questions for which there is no answer. All peoples on earth have found their way to God, to some kind of God, to some answer to the universe that is above and outside themselves.

It is not the idea of God that sets us apart in the history of humanity. It is the kind of God in which we choose to believe that in the end makes all the difference. And each of us fashions a private God, the face of whom shapes our own.

Some believe, for instance, in a God of wrath and so themselves become wrathful at others as a result. Some believe in a God who is indifferent to the world and, when they find themselves alone—as all of us do at some time or another—they shrivel up and die inside from the indifference they feel in the world around them.

Some believe in a God who makes traffic lights turn green and so become the children of magical coincidence in a world crying out for clear-eyed, hardheaded, responsible shapers of this clay called life.

Some believe in a God of laws, and crumble in spirit and psyche when they themselves break those laws or else become even more stern in demanding from others standards they themselves cannot keep. They conceive of God as the manipulator of the universe rather than its ground. God, they hold, is the part of the scene that lies behind the objects in the forefront. They project on to God humanity's own small desires and indignities and needs.

All have failed me

I have known all of those Gods in my own life, and they have all failed me.

I have learned that law-keeping did not satisfy my need for meaning. I learned that to be properly wicked it was not necessary to break the law—just to keep it to the letter! I have learned that the fear of wrath did not seduce me to love. I have learned that God, the distant doer of unpredictable and arbitrary magic, failed to engage or enliven my soul. I have learned that life was surely about far more important things than that. If the question, then, is "Who is God for me in the year 2000?" my answer has to be, "God is not the God I thought I knew in 1950."

One of the best things I was ever taught about God was by a philosophy professor who told us that we could not "think" God. And he was obviously right, though clearly, think God we did—and aplenty. In my own case, God has been a changing, moving, inviting, disturbing, and totally engrossing mystery, and the more I thought about God, it seemed, the less I knew God at all.

I have feared the God of judgment and have been judgmental of others. I have used God to get me through life. I have called the intolerable "God's will" and called our failure to stop evil God's failure to stop evil. I have expected God to be the crutch that would make the unbearable bearable. As a result, I have often failed to take steps to change life either for myself or others when injustice masked itself as God's will and oppression as God's judgment.

I have thought about God "out there" and become blind to the God within me. And so, thinking of God as far away, I have failed to make God present to others who were in my presence.

I have, in other words, allowed God to be mediated to me through images of God foreign to the very idea of God:

> God the puppeteer, who created free will but takes it back when it gets inconvenient;
> God the potentate, whose interest is self-love;
> God the persecutor, who created life to trap it in its own ignorance;
> God the mighty male to whom obedience, subservience, and deference were the only proper responses, and in whose being women were apparent only by their absence.

I have come to the conclusion, after a lifetime of looking for God, that a divinity such as any of these is simply a graven image of ourselves, not a God big enough to believe in.

All of those images, ironically, actually blocked the image of the presence of God in life for me. All of them made a mockery of the very definition of God—the fullness of being—who, having created

us, wills us well and not woe, good and not grief, and all of us fullness
of life, not some of us inert and invisible nothingness.

The God in whom we choose to believe determines the rest of
life for us. In our conception of the nature of God lies the kernel of
the spiritual life. Surely, no one really believes that this conference is
about *God* at 2000. This conference is about *us* at 2000!

Made in the image of God, we grow in the image of the God we
make for ourselves. They told us that God was creator and judge. They
drew pictures to prove the point. But they forgot to tell us what they
could not draw. They neglected to tell us what the philosophy professor knew: God is what we cannot think and what we cannot *not*
think at the same time.

We have, obviously, in our attempt to understand God as personal,
configured the Godhead to be a person writ larger than ourselves. We
have seen in that limited conception both the best and the worst, the
most limitless and the most limited of ourselves. To make this partial-
ity an absolute warps both God and us. I substitute my own limitations
for the limitlessness of God.

I learned as life went by that the God I make will be the God I
seek, the spiritual life I live, and the quality of my own heart. Until I
discover the God in whom I myself believe, then, until I unmask the
God who lives in my own heart, regardless of the panoply of other
God images around me, I will never understand another thing about
my own life. Or, as Woody Allen said, "Confidence is what we have
until we understand the problem."

I knew, when I looked back, that when my God was a harsh judge,
I lived in a guilt so unquenchable that it blocked the fullness of whatever goodness might be in me and most of the hope in me as well. I
knew I could not possibly measure up even to the smallness of the
God I had made.

I myself have lived in those boxes of sins where the rules I kept and
the rituals I practiced were my gods. They were more important to me
than the people I met who, helpless as they were, could do nothing but
wait for God to work through me and through my devotion to God on

their behalf. Unlike the God of the prodigal son, this small God of mine shut doors in the face of the ones not as plumb, not as rigid as I, so that in my rigidity I skewed the very spiritual course I was intent to follow.

The checklists and the dos and don'ts had become my God, until those gods waxed and waned and disappeared into the dust out of which they had been formed.

In the period of my life when my God became Holy Nothingness—not so much imaginary as simply a philosophical question of no great immediate interest and even less conviction—I lived a life of cosmic loneliness. The great questions of life became: What is it all about? Why bother? And who cares anyway?

I discovered the chasm of the soul that comes when God is too high to care and too far away to notice; when God the vending machine did not answer in the way I wanted; when God the judge let evil go by unchallenged; when my God was taunter and bully, who tweaked and teased me with temptations rather than give me the experiences I needed to bring me to what Julian of Norwich had experienced, the very heights of mystical consciousness. I was struggling through life impaled on the pin of a grinning giant called God!

Not thinking God, but knowing God

I learned as life went on that clearly the professor was correct: I could not think God. But, I have now learned, the professor was also incorrect at the same time. Not to be able to think about God is only to make God unthinkable; it is not to make God unreal. The great spiritual truth, I learned over the years, is that, indeed, we cannot think God. We can only know God. And when we do think God into some single, separate, stultifying shape, it is only a sign that we now run the risk of knowing God less and less.

Each of these separate dimensions of God—justice and law and reason and omnipotence and a kind of "tsk-tsking" love at a distance—marks a stage of my own life. Each of them has been a highway marker through a complex of religious practices. Each of them has been good for the sake of the focus they gave me but false when they

became an end in themselves and dimmed the sacramental nature—
the divine depths—of the rest of life.

I searched for God and found the God who was a tribal God, the
God who was a Catholic God, the God who was on our side not
theirs, the God who was white and American and male—definitely
male—the God they called key, door, wind, spirit, dove, and rock, but
never, never mother! But over the years, faced with one question after
another—*What was it to be a woman? What was it to step into outer space?
What was it to see goodness where once I had been told only faithlessness
abounded?*—I became more and more convinced that God was to be
found in other places and that only the search itself could possibly save
me from the worst consequences of each.

I have seen God grow. Or maybe I have seen me grow and couldn't
tell the difference.

I have abandoned God the stern father who had no time for
human nonsense and little time for women, either. I have abandoned
"God the cloud-sitter" who keeps count of our childish stumbles
toward spiritual adulthood in order to exact fierce retribution from
humans for being human. And I have seen all those fragments of the
face of God dissolve into the mist of impossibility.

I am more and more convinced that those Gods do not exist, never
did exist, must not exist if God is really God.

But when such small ideas die, with what great thoughts shall we
replace them?

I have become sure that if all I know about God is that my God is
the fullness of life and the consummation of hope, the light on the
way, and the light at the end, then I will live my life in the consciousness of God and of goodness everywhere, obscure at times, perhaps,
but never wholly lacking.

God as Cosmic Unity and Everlasting Light

So now God, that old rascal, is doing it again. I am moving in my
heart from God as a trophy to be won, or a master, however benign,
to be pacified, to God as cosmic unity and everlasting light.

The change has been gradual but very, very clear. It has come at the juncture of five divides, all seemingly separate, but all of a piece: spiritual tradition, personal experience, science, globalism, and feminism. These have all come together in my life to show me a God whom I cannot think, but do deeply know, to be real. I have learned from them all to know a greater God than I had been given. Let me explain.

God always before our eyes

The spiritual tradition that guides me is an ancient one: In the Rule of Benedict of Nursia (a Catholic document written in the sixth century and still the way of life for thousands of monastics today) chapter seven—"On Humility"—sums up Benedict's spiritual theology. In light of the spirituality of the last several hundred years, what he says is at least startling if not unsettling.

The first degree of humility, the first step on the way to God, is to have always before our eyes what the ancients called the fear of God—what we know as the sense of God, the awe of God, the awareness of God, the presence of God.[26]

The religious culture of Benedict's time was immersed in merit theology, a theology that sought deliverance from damnation by earning God. So many masses equal so much union with God, so many rosaries equal so many units of God, so many penances and sacrifices and formulas of the faith equal so much fullness of God. Into this religious culture came an astounding revelation. The first step to union with God is knowing that you already have God, you already enjoy God, and you already contain within yourself the life that is God.

Both the Jewish mystic Isaac Luria (1534–1572) and the Catholic theologian Pierre Teilhard de Chardin (1881–1955) speak of the sparks of God—the residue of the creator in all of us—as common to the entire human race. The idea goes back to Moses at a flaming bush; to Jesus aglow on a mountaintop; to Benedict's first degree of humility that teaches us the grandeur of us all; to the mystic Julian of Norwich, who saw God as nurturing mother and "all that is" in an acorn. It links us in turn to the here and now, to a kind of spirituality that breaks down barriers and jumps boundaries. This is a spirituality in which I know that wherever I am, whatever my state of mind, God is the spirit with me and the life in me. God is there for the taking. God is the air I breathe, and God is the path I take. God is the womb in which I live. As the Zen proverb reads: "If enlightenment is not where you are standing, where will you look?" This was the Benedictine spirituality, steeped in the Jewish and Christian scriptures, that changed my awareness of the living God as alive around me, existing beyond me, and breathing within me.

There were other things as well. Personal experience, science, globalism, and feminism came to crumble, wash away, and replace a God made small by puny ideas cast in puny images.

An experience of intense light

My ideas about God shook themselves free of legal lists and the golden calves of denominationalism, maleness, and race. It took another half a lifetime to come to trust them. As a young teenager, kneeling in a dark cathedral one night, with no illumination in the church but the sanctuary lamp, I had an experience of intense light. I was thirteen years old and totally convinced that, whatever it was and wherever it came from, the light was God. Perhaps it was a good janitor working late, or a bad switch that did not work at all, or a startling insight given to a young woman, given gratuitously. I did not know then and I do not know now. But I did know that the light was God and that God was light.

I was never able to forget that experience, nor did I ever talk about it, until this very moment. And I do so now because I am here in private conversation with a few thousand of my most intimate friends, and then only because I was confronted by the honest question, "Who is God for you?" I have few classical answers, but it demands an honest response.

After that experience, whenever God was shrunk to meet someone's then current need to control or frighten or cajole me, whenever

God the vending machine or God the theological Santa Claus did not give me what I wanted, or whenever God the judge let evil go by unchallenged, I knew now that God was bigger than these gods, because I was never able to stop feeling the unshaped, uncontrolled, and undiminished light.

For me, as an adult, two different texts confirmed the image of God that I learned that night in the cathedral and lived for years in the presence of God in a Benedictine community. The first text that called me to images beyond images was the Hebrew-Christian scriptures, an ancient commentary and testimony on God's ways in the world. The scriptures showed me the God who would not test Job; who debated with Abraham about the degree of sinlessness it would take to save the city, and lost; the God whose own identity was revealed to Moses simply, profoundly, as "I Am Who I Am," "I Will Be What I Will Be," and to Jonah as "mercy upon mercy upon mercy," and in the Jesus of the Mount of Transfiguration bathed in light. This was a God without a face of any color or gender, a God who came in fire and light, God with us— Emmanuel—but unseen, God with me, but hidden in the obvious. That God, I knew, lived in the light. And the light, I could feel, was inside me.

The second text was a tiny little book by Jeanne Pierre de Caussade called *Abandonment to Divine Providence*. It brought me beyond the God of the distant and the partial, the punitive and the parental. It kept an ancient stream of thought alive under the avalanche of legalism, denominationalism, and doctrinal rules. The title of the book sounds like some kind of professional quietism or personal masochism, but it brought the distant God as close to me as the minute I am in. Then all the thinking stopped and the knowing began, and the light burned the images away.

After that growing awareness of the immersing presence of God, I became conscious of two other present and obvious, but long-standing threats to traditional religious belief. Each became a spiritual revelation to me that was both logical and undeniable.

The material in the spiritual and the spiritual in the material

The first burst of insight was science, once the champion of the "material" and the skeptic of the spiritual. Science had made the split between the two seem irreconcilable. But then scientists unexpectedly discovered that the only difference between solids and space was the degree to which the same atoms that composed both were packed more or less closely together. The old line—the heretofore uncompromising dividing line between matter and spirit—had suddenly blurred. How could we really separate the two? So why not the material in the spiritual and the spiritual in the material? I learned, too, that the God who could not be verified was no greater an assumption than the scientific "facts" of modern physics, astronomy, or cosmology. These could not be verified experientially either, unless you know someone who has walked to Mars with a pedometer in her hand.

The mathematical findings of quantum physics, chaos theory, and the Big Bang forced classical scientific theory to turn in a different direction. The limits of knowledge ran out. Knowledge of the unlimited consumed us, and broke open our spirits to spiritual things greater than ourselves. A universe which, in 1900, we had taught with confidence had one galaxy, the Milky Way, now revealed to the telescope's eye in the year 2000 that there were at least forty billion galaxies out there. In such a world newly revealed as this, even the agnostic physicist Stephen Hawking asked in wonder who or what it was that "breathes fire into the equations?"[27] Who or what is the beginning behind the universe? The energy in the eternal expansion?

Suddenly science was a great spiritual teacher for me. Science became the guide to a God far greater than the God of petty sins, trivial traps, and privatized religion. God was the God of the universe whose creating life lives in us, in me and in others, and in the stars, and whose light is bringing us home.

A new kind of cognitive dissonance

The second burst of insight across the sensors of my soul that changed the image of God for me was far less ethereal than science and cosmology. The melting of national boundaries and the free flow of peoples and ideas across the globe introduced for me a new kind of cognitive dissonance. The white, male, Catholic, American God was suddenly suspect. Were all these others—over four-fifths of the world—really "Godless," without revelation, without any or all truth? Globalism, I came to realize, was a less startling, less dramatic revelation of the presence of God. Perhaps in the end it was, at least for me, an even more revealing one than scientific equations could ever be.

Sprung from the Catholic ghetto, however good that may have been in my spiritual formation, I found God at work everywhere, revealed everywhere, and known everywhere. An old joke tells about God warning every new person at the gates of Paradise to tiptoe past Room 10 on the way to their heavenly quarters, because the Catholics were in Room 10, and they thought they were the only people there. The joke took on new meaning for me. So did Jesus' insight that in the house of God there were many dwelling places (John 14:2), Benedict's vision of having seen "the whole world in a single ray of light," and the injunction of Vatican Council II to "accept whatever was true" in other religions. Clearly, then, something was happening to me. I had learned the greatest truth of all. God was bigger than parochialism. God had many faces. God had many names. God was a magnet in many hearts, all of which, according to the Parliament of the World's Religions meeting in Cape Town in December 1999, embraced a common global ethic: not to lie, not to steal, not to kill, and not to exploit others sexually. Or to put it in more religious terms: to hold all life sacred, to honor every truth, to deal with all people justly, and to love all life rightly. Clearly, the God of differences spoke in one voice, under whatever form that God might be enshrined, anywhere, everywhere.

So, as my world became smaller, God became infinitely larger. God became present for me not just everywhere, but in everyone, and in many ways. God became present in a cataract of otherness, the likes of which I had never dreamed. God, as Anselm said in the eleventh century, had become for me "that than which nothing greater can be thought."

The third burst of insight was ecofeminism, the growing awareness that both an androcentric (male centered) and an anthropocen-
tric (human centered) world are insufficient, even warped, explanations
of life if God is really the fullness of being and no single being is the
fullness of God.

When the question is "Are women fully human?" and the scientific
answer is a resounding yes; when the scriptural explanation of creation
is Adam's declaration that Eve is "bone of my bone, flesh of my flesh,"
someone just like me; when human beings at the top of the food chain
will be the first to go if the planet is degraded; when nothing on earth
is dependent on human life for its existence and humans are dependent for theirs on everything else on the planet; and if God, to be God,
must be pure spirit, then Augustine's hierarchy of being—maleness and
a God made in a male image—has got to be at best suspect, at the least
incomplete, and in the end bogus.

This male construct of a male God in a male-centered world is no
picture of God at all. God is not maleness magnified. God is life without end: all life, in everything, in everyone, in men and women, and
in women and men. The light of the divine shines everywhere and
has no gender, no single pronoun, no one image.

Life for me has been one long struggle between those limited and
myopic images of God and the lifelong prevailing sense of a far greater
experience, a more encompassing presence called God.

If the question is: "Who is God for you in the year 2000?" then for
me at least—in the face of new glimpses into the universe, the findings of science, the continuing insights of an ancient tradition, the
piercing experience of light, the many faces of God around the globe,
and the revelations of ecofeminism—the answer is certainly "God is
not now who God was for me in 1950." The God at the other swing
of my trapeze is fierce but formless presence, undying light in darkness, eternal limitlessness, common consciousness in all creation, an
inclusiveness, greater than doctrines or denominations, who calls me
beyond and out of my limits.

The only proper response to that, as far as I am concerned, is
"Thank God. Thank God. Thank God."

I have learned clearly that in this new world I must allow no one to draw too small a God for me.

We must know that we have already found what we seek. "Not one. Not two."

And we must realize that, for the sake of the people, for the sake of the planet, for the sake of the empowering presence of God in an increasingly godless world, we must search for God with all the new lights we have.

As Augustine concluded at the end of his own struggle between the intellectual and the religious images of God, "It is better to find you, God, and leave the questions unanswered, than to find answers without finding you."

Follow-up Questions

JC = Joan Chittister   Q = Questioner   M = Moderator

M You talked about the fact that the God we believe in really matters. Do you see any promising signs? Do you think things are changing?

JC This conference is a sign. I never dreamed that someone would put this kind of energy into this kind of conference. To have an interest in this question of God and to be willing to discuss it together outside of our denominational chapter meetings—if that is not a sign of God's presence, what is!

Q How do you personally maintain and sustain your search, living within an institution that does not always honor where you go or the search itself?

JC There are two answers, both of which are honest. I have struggled through the question, as you will know. First, I am a social psychologist by training. So I take seriously the power of symbol, language, development, and formation. I believe we are standing in a period when we are asking too much of our churches. We live in a world where people are coming back to the simple concepts I laid out in my talk. They are finding a struggle between religion and spirituality. But religion and spirituality are not synonyms. If my own spiritual life is beginning to be nurtured in other streams than mine, am I therefore unfaithful to my religion? I would argue: absolutely not.

Second, I see my own tradition as a repository of the best in the spiritual struggle across the history of Western civilization. The institution in that struggle has often been out of synch in terms of time. Ask Martin Luther. But we eventually catch up. What's four hundred years among friends? [*Laughter*] But that is not a uniquely Catholic sin. [*Applause*]

Q   Thank you for your courage in telling us that God is not male. How can those of us who are pastors work to change people's image of God, so that they can see God as something other than male?

JC   This is the key question in my opinion. Ecofeminism is both a philosophy and a theology that must germinate. When I look at studies in ecology today, I have yet to see someone point to the link between patriarchy and the destruction of the planet. A feminist value system is other than a patriarchal value system. (Brothers, please understand, I am not equating patriarchy and maleness.) Feminists come in two genders. Feminist and female are also not the same word. I bet there are one or two patriarchal women sniffing around in here! [*Laughter and applause*] The patriarchal woman has embodied in herself this patriarchal value system and believes her own inferiority. She has bought the language of the oppressor. The black community knows this.

Social scientists have done longitudinal studies on the effects of oppression on the personality of the oppressed. It is my feminist brothers who have given me a right to hope and believe that what I see is true. Otherwise all you have is a new chauvinism. You can't just replace male chauvinism with a female version. [*Applause*] Tokenism is the strategy of an institution to take a few of the minority from the outside to the inside, and to keep the rest of the minority on the outside, while they can go on looking good. You have to move away from tokenism, flee it like the plague. One woman on a committee is not equality. People say to me, "But Sister Joan, we just can't rush into this." I say, "Well, honey, is two thousand years enough tippie-toe for you?" [*Laughter*]

How do we pastor in these situations? We simply refuse tokenism and we equalize. We equalize the images on the altar, in the committee structures, and in language. We break those boundaries and taboos that hold us. In some Christian churches when you get to the distribution of the Eucharist and when that distribution is under two forms, bread and wine, you would be amazed how consistently the men distribute the bread and the women the wine. Now if Jesus is present indeed, whole and entire under both species, then, "Father, feel free. There's a chalice over in this corner." [*Laughter*] You pastor by structuring, changing language, bringing people together in small groups to discuss literature that brings another consciousness, an inclusive consciousness, to the questions. There hasn't been a book published in the last twenty years that uses the old sexist language. Isn't it a shame that it is publishers that are leading the way and not the church? [*Applause*]

Q How have you been able to reconcile the importance of voice in feminism and of silence or humility in religion?

JC Humility and humiliation are not the same thing. We Catholics come from a spiritual tradition of humiliation in the name of spiritual development. That has nothing whatever to do with the virtue of humility. The word itself comes from the Latin *humus*, meaning earth. It means knowing who you are and who you are not. Being good in some things does not give you control in everything. It does not give you the right not to hear someone else's voice. It also does not give you the right to be silent when you have a voice to raise. Humility is what enables the person to do these things. Humble people have no fear of failure, because all they have is themselves. You must give what you have, take nothing that doesn't belong to you, and suppress no one in the giving of your own gifts. [*Applause*]

Q Expand a little on the God who is within, and how we are to know this God as opposed to thinking this God.

JC The God who is within is that impulse toward good, the moral compass of the heart. We know that God by moving always in a straight line set by that compass. That compass points always to ultimate truth. You know when you are lying. You know when your life is a lie. You know when the way you treat others is a lie. There is no one in this audience today who hasn't worked under someone who was lying about their superiority, and in order to maintain the lie kept repressing everybody else. The God who is within liberates us to be the best that we can possibly be, to see goodness where it is, to allow ourselves to be drawn toward it, to live out of it, and to draw it to ourselves with a passion. When I know that I have been prompted beyond my smallness, I know the God within. When I know that I have learned to see beyond old personal horizons, I know the God within. And when I finally come to see that God in the other, I know the God within, because the God within is always pulling me towards you. I don't have to think that. I only have to do that. [*Applause*]

Q   What does Jesus Christ the man mean to you as a Christian in your understanding of God?

JC   Well, I love Jesus. I become more and more immersed in the one who is Jesus of Nazareth and Jesus the Christ. We struggle to separate mythology and meaning in our understanding of that Jesus. In Jesus the divine sparks that are in all of us have come to fullness, to as close a reflection of the nature of God as we can see on earth. Jesus the male is my brother. He is the most feminist male I know, and from him I take great strength. [*Applause*]

5 God: The Reality to Serve, Love, and Know
Seyyed Hossein Nasr

Seyyed Hossein Nasr is University Professor of Islamic Studies at George Washington University in Washington, D.C. The author of more than twenty books and 250 articles, he is one of the foremost scholars of Islam in the world today. Coeditor of the two-volume *The History of Islamic Philosophy,* he and his work are the subject of a whole volume in *The Library of Living Philosophers.* He has given the Gifford Lectures, the most prestigious lecture series in religion in the world. He has also won the Templeton Award for the best course in America in religion and science.

His many books reflect his broad interests: the history, philosophy, science, and spirituality of Islam; religion, mysticism, and science; modern and primordial worldviews; the sacred and nature. He has written works in four different languages, and they have been translated into more than ten languages. His more then twenty titles include: *Ideals and Realities of Islam; An Introduction to Islamic Cosmological Doctrines; Islam and the Plight of Modern Man; Islamic Art and Spirituality; The Islamic Intellectual Tradition in Persia; Man and Nature: The Spiritual Crisis of Modern Man; Religion in the Order of Nature;* and *Knowledge and the Sacred* (the Gifford Lectures).

Nasr grew up in Iran and came to the United States for college and graduate school. His degrees reflect his strong interest in science and religion. He earned his bachelor's degree in physics and mathematics from the Massachusetts Institute of Technology, his master's in geology and geophysics from Harvard, and his doctor's degree in the history of science and philosophy, also from Harvard. He returned to Iran to teach at Tehran University, where he was a full professor when he left the country in 1979 to teach in the United States. Before becoming University Professor of Islamic Studies at George Washington, he held teaching appointments at Temple, Princeton, and Harvard.

Bismi'Llāh al-Raḥmīn al-Rahīm

In the Islamic tradition all legitimate daily acts commence with this sentence: "In the Name of God, the All Good, the Compassionate." Surely I could not begin a conference on God without beginning with this statement. It is also the profoundest commentary upon the divine nature as it relates not only to humanity but also to the whole of creation. The two divine names, *al-Rahmān* and *al-Rahīm,* are both derived from the root *rḥm* that is also the root of the word *rahim,* meaning womb. (The similar word for "womb" in Hebrew, *rehem,* belongs to the same linguistic family as Arabic.) The world and we who are in it are born from the womb of the divine mercy, without which we would not even exist. The very substance of cosmic reality is the "breath of the Compassionate" *(nafas al-Rahmān),* as the Sufis assert. To name God's names—*Rahmān* and *Rahīm*—is to remember that mercy from which we have issued forth and in which we live, whether or not we are aware of our real natures. To that mercy we ultimately return, if we remember who we are and accept that great "trust of faith" to which we must consent by our free will as human beings.

From the point of view of traditional teachings the relation between the divine source and the creation rooted in this mercy is one that transcends time and becoming. Time is but one of the conditions of our terrestrial mode of existence. The title of this conference, "God at 2000," should not for one moment imply a temporal condition imposed on that metahistorical relation. Whatever we may comprehend by the term "God at 2000," it is much more important to understand that the world at 2000, like every other world at any particular moment of time, is a reflection of a metatemporal reality. It is rooted in that reality, whatever may be our passing understanding of things. Perhaps, then, rather than speaking of God at 2000 one should speak of the world at 2000 "in" God, for multiplicity is at every moment mysteriously immersed in God.

Speaking of God Personally

The organizers of this conference have asked the speakers to speak of God from an experiential and personal point of view, which is usually not my preference. I would rather have spoken of God in a manner that transcends the personal idiosyncrasies of individual existence. Nevertheless, having accepted the invitation to speak here at the beginning of the new Christian millennium and about the most important of all subjects, I am obliged to begin by saying something about my background and education, since they are related to my understanding of the subject at hand. But my purpose most of all is to write a few humble words about God from the point of view of the Islamic tradition to which I belong.

Early upbringing

I was born and brought up in a Muslim family in Persia, from where I hail originally. My family was one in which the reality of Islam was very strong. We felt and experienced the dimension of transcendence and the reality of God everywhere. My childhood years were inseparable from the constant observation of the sacred rites of the daily prayers and the ever-present chanting of the Qur'an, which for Muslims is the verbatim revelation of God and God's very word. My maternal family came from a long line of famous religious scholars or 'ulamā.' My father, in addition to being a great scholar and thinker, was also devoted to Sufism, the inner or mystical dimension of Islam. Sufism is the heart of the Islamic revelation. Unfortunately, however, some in the West seek to divorce it from Islam and propagate it in a diluted fashion that is far from its authentic reality.

I remember that at the very young age of five or six, in addition to getting me to memorize certain verses and chapters of the Qur'an, my parents guided me to learn and memorize some of the poems of the greatest Persian Sufi poets, such as Jalāl ad-Dīn Rūmī and Muḥammad Shams al-Dīn Ḥāfiẓ. Within their incredible spiritual depth these poems often sang of the unity of religious truth, of the universality of religion, and of crossing religious frontiers. They constituted my first lessons in what has now come to be known as religious dialogue. They planted within my mind and soul the seed of a tree that was to grow in later years and become an important axis of my soul and a central concern of my mind. I will quote just one poem from memory by the supreme troubadour of love—both human and divine—in the Persian language, Ḥāfiz, a poem that I had already known before the age of ten. Its imperfect translation is as follows:

> In love there is no difference between the Christian monastery and the temple of the Magi,
>> Wherever there is anything, there is the light of the face of the beloved.

I was brought up in such a tradition, and I have never left it. At a very young age an intimacy with the divine reality was created in my soul. This reality was and remains for me at once all encompassing and all caring, universal and yet the source of particular sacred forms, all loving and yet awesome. In my understanding of God the reality of the divine *tremendum*—the majesty of God—has always been combined with his love, mercy, and, of course, his beauty. The divine names of majesty (*al-Jalāl*) and beauty (*al-Jamāl*) complement each other perfectly in the Islamic perspective. There are verses of the Qur'an that speak of God as the utterly other, the transcendent, the beyond, or that which has no like. Islam, like Judaism, emphasizes the oneness of God above all else. And yet there are other verses of the Qur'an that speak of the intimacy of God with us and of his love. One of the divine names is *al-Wudūd*, which means precisely love. The Qur'an speaks also of the mercy of God that "embraces all things." God is closer to us than our jugular vein, and "wherever we turn, there is the face of God."

In a profound sense the journey of the soul to God is an oscillation between these two poles of majesty and beauty, farness and nearness, involving a movement both horizontal and vertical without which no spiritual journey would be complete. An awareness of these two aspects—the divine reality and the proper orientation of our soul and indeed the whole of our being—is necessary if we are to realize the divine origin of our existence, fulfill the purpose of our journey here on earth, and smell the fragrance of the divine reality. God is both transcendent and immanent. We must comprehend that both of these dimensions are in God. But it is also necessary to add that we can gain no sense of the immanent dimension without that of the transcendent.

Secondary and higher education

Returning to my personal life, I was sent to the West to continue my studies when I was quite young. Thus I was plucked from the protective surroundings of Persia and my family before my mental outlook was completely formed. Coming to America did not, however, mean immediate immersion in a secular environment. Before going to Massachusetts Institute of Technology, I underwent the second part of my secondary education at the Peddie School in New Jersey, a Baptist school where, despite being a Muslim, I had to attend church every Sunday. That experience came to complement my later intellectual study of Christianity and was valuable despite the strangeness of its form. The experience strengthened the flame of the love for Christ that is inculcated in the hearts of Muslims in general and was emphasized in my own upbringing in particular. I continued, of course, to view Christ as the greatest prophet before the Prophet of Islam, but not as an incarnation of God, which Islam rejects, since it bases its understanding of God on the absolute itself rather than on its manifestation. The great love for 'Īsā ibn Maryam, that is, Jesus son of Mary, as the Qur'an calls him, has remained in my heart to this day and in fact has grown deeper because of that early existential encounter with Christianity as well as from much later study and meditation.

It was also at the Peddie School that the gifts God had given me in the sciences and especially mathematics became manifest. I received some of the highest scores ever achieved in both local and national mathematics tests. All my teachers therefore advised me to become a scientist. I also felt enthusiastic about studying physics, the mother of modern sciences, and I went to MIT with great joy and in expectation of investigating the nature of physical reality. It took me many years and much more introspection to realize that what I really wanted to be was a *physikos* in the sense given to it by Parmenides. Considered by many as the father of Western philosophy, Parmenides taught that a *physikos* was a person who sought to understand the nature of things in an ontological sense and not simply in appearance. While only a sophomore, I discovered that modern physics does not in fact deal with the nature of reality, even with physical reality in itself, as I had thought. Much reading in the modern philosophy of science, most of it based on positivism, confirmed this fact for me. As I have written in my intellectual autobiography,[28] it was a lecture and later a more personal meeting in Cambridge with Bertrand Russell, the famous British philosopher, that proved to be a critical turning point for me. He asserted that physics deals only with pointer readings and mathematical structures, not with the nature of physical reality itself in the ontological sense.

Graduate studies

After that encounter I decided to leave the field of science once and for all. But I decided to complete my degree before making a change. I remained, therefore, in the field of the sciences for a few more years, completing my bachelor's degree in physics and mathematics at MIT and my master's degree in geology and geophysics at Harvard. Meanwhile, in parallel with my scientific studies I was studying philosophy and the history of science and finally turned to these subjects for my doctoral work. The whole experience of modern science, and especially the positivistic philosophy of science then being propagated, as well as the whole agnostic and to some extent atheistic climate in which I was studying, provided a major challenge to my theocentric worldview. But being the type of person that I was, I could not leave any form of knowledge presented to me alone, but had to study and seek its meaning as well as examine its claims.

For many years, starting with my time at MIT, I studied Descartes, Hume, Kant, Hegel, and other Western philosophers up to those of the contemporary period, including Whitehead. The immersion in the world of doubt cultivated by the mainstream of postmedieval European philosophy shook the framework of my intellectual world, but it did not affect my faith in God nor that inner and intimate relationship with the divine that I had experienced since childhood. Nevertheless, it created a major crisis within my mind and soul. I am in fact one of the first from the East to have faced such a crisis fully without succumbing to the tenets of modernism. My response, after some period of anguish, meditation, study, and introspection, was to reject totally the whole adventure of Renaissance humanism and Enlightenment rationalism, in other words the very foundations of modernism. Since then my intellectual life has been dedicated to providing, on the basis of traditional teachings, especially but not exclusively those of Islam, answers to the challenges posed by modernism and queries that arise from its rejection. I have sought to discuss the consequence of severing the link between reason and intellect in the sense used by St. Thomas and the reduction of the latter to the former. I have dealt extensively with the consequences of the anthropomorphism prevalent in the West that makes an absolute of the terrestrial human state and makes the human being "the measure of all things." In this sense modern science is completely anthropomorphic, since it is based solely on the human senses and human reason, no matter how much it seeks to exclude man from a cosmology limited to the physical realm but extended to vast expanses of space and time.

A Philosophy Rooted in the Divine Reality

At the moment of my intellectual crisis I was avidly reading Western philosophical works, and also looking anywhere that I could for intellectual guidance with which to reestablish the certitude on which my whole outlook was based until my MIT years. Then I discovered the works of the authors who are called the traditionalists or expositors of primordial wisdom and the perennial philosophy, foremost among them René Guénon, Ananda K. Coomaraswamy, and Frithjof Schuon. These authors opened many doors for me and provided the crucial knowledge based on certainty that I was seeking. They also provided the in-depth criticism of the modern world that allowed me to see clearly the nature of that world and to formulate succinctly ideas concerning that world, the meaning of which had been still ambiguous and tentative in my mind until then. They presented pure metaphysical knowledge, to which my mind was drawn like a moth to the candle. And they opened my eyes to the vast world that was both non-Islamic and non-Western, embracing both the Far East and Hindu India.

A. K. Coomaraswamy was perhaps the most outstanding and certainly the most authentic expositor of Hinduism and Buddhism in this country in the first part of the 20th century. By chance I came to meet his widow. (Coomaraswamy had died in 1947, some five years before.) This meeting in turn gained for me access to the incomparable Coomaraswamy library in which I spent countless hours for several years reading about various traditions, especially Hinduism, Taoism, and Buddhism. Although art was not my field, as a result of the influence of the works of Coomaraswamy I took nearly every course on Hindu and Buddhist art at Harvard. There I met nearly every important person in these domains, including scholars such as D. T. Suzuki, who was working in the field of Eastern religions and art. These studies and experiences had a great effect in reconfirming on an intellectual plane what I had already intuited as a young man, namely, that the splendor of the face of God is to be found in quite different religious contexts.

A single truth spoken in different languages

Wherever I journeyed intellectually, if I found in that world a philosophy rooted in the divine reality, I felt at home there. I soon came to realize that my spiritual home is wherever the divine resides, no matter in what form it had manifested itself or in what language it had said "I." This realization was related in its intellectual aspect to the discovery of the perennial philosophy, *philosophia perennis*, which the traditional authors expounded, and which became and remains my philosophical outlook. The perennial philosophy is based on a set of universal truths that lay, its followers believe, at the heart of all authentic religions and traditional philosophies. One might assert that there is but a single truth, spoken in different languages, that constitutes the various worlds of sacred form. Moreover, this oneness does not imply that either differences on the formal plane or the preciousness of each sacred form are inconsequential, different though each is from other forms. The perennial philosophy sees unity on the level of inner or transcendent reality, not on the formal plane, and it does not ever confuse unity with uniformity. My lecture today does not deal with comparative religion but with God. It is necessary, however, to point to this central issue, because in the contemporary world other views of God can and often do affect our own views.

It was also during my years of formal university education that I embarked upon the spiritual path within the Sufi tradition. This is a matter about which I prefer not to speak publicly; but for the sake of honesty I need to mention it, especially since the Sufi path has determined the conditions of my lifelong quest for spiritual realization and has provided the light and guidance for it. The quest for God has been at the heart of my life since my twenties. That quest has remained central throughout all my other activities from teaching and writing to founding or running academic, cultural, and educational institutions. What I have to say about God is the fruit not only of the studies and the experiences that I have outlined briefly, it has been above all of the path that has led me to him. The result of following the path is dependent not only on the efforts of the traveler upon the path, but above all on divine grace and affirmation.

There is a well-known Taoist saying according to which, "Those who know do not speak, and those who speak do not know." This saying refers to the ineffable nature of the hidden mysteries about which the wise must keep silent, with mouths shut. (This is what the root of the word mysticism precisely signifies.) The saying also refers to the ineffability of the supreme knowledge of God, to which others in this conference have also referred. All that we can say about God is little in relation to what we cannot utter about him, because human language cannot contain truths that only symbols or silence itself can transmit, together with what the Sufis call "indication" or *ishārah*. The most eloquent discourse on God leads ultimately to silence, and the silent and yet so eloquent divine presence is itself the most powerful means of conveying the reality of God.

A journey to southern India

Since several participants of this conference have taken recourse in the ancient art of storytelling, it is perhaps not inappropriate to recount here a personal story that is relevant to what we are talking about. In 1971 when I was living in Iran, I made a journey to southern India. My many earlier trips had been to the north. Since I was going to Madras, I requested a meeting with the Śankaracharya of Kanćipuram, at that time one of the supreme spiritual figures of India, who was in the direct lineage of the great Śankara, and who lived near Madras. He was a venerable sage who moved about with a large retinue like a king, but who lived at the same time in extreme simplicity. On the day of the appointment I was driven to Kanći and taken to a wonderful orchard in the middle of which they had placed a beautiful carpet for me to sit on. Wearing traditional Islamic dress, I sat crosslegged on the carpet awaiting the coming of the great Hindu master. After a few minutes he entered the orchard holding the staff of a *sannyāsin*. He came to within some ten yards of me and then squatted on the ground without his staff touching the earth. A disciple accompanying him greeted me on behalf of the master who, he explained, was observing a fast of silence. Being an untouchable from the point of view of Hindu law, which I, of course, honored greatly, I could not come closer to the Hindu master nor could he to me. And so we looked each other in the eye for several minutes in utter silence. Then he smiled and made some signs with his hands to his disciple, who then said to me, "The master says that he wishes to tell his Persian friend [that is, myself] how happy he is that the understanding of the reality of God in Advaita and Sufism is the same." Here was a discourse on God at the highest level carried out in silence and also the most profound religious dialogue I have ever carried out with the representative of another religion, although not a single word was exchanged between us.

Those who claim to speak about God must always respect this principial[29] silence that must even penetrate into our speech. We come from silence and return to it. We are like waves of the sea that issue from the calm waters and ultimately return to that infinite calm and quietude. This having been said, it is necessary to state also that the Word created all things and that our speech, itself a divine gift, has the power to express in some ways the highest realities that the heart and intelligence are capable of knowing. The classical theological and philosophical principle known as adequation also holds true for language. Human language is capable of expressing truths about the divine; otherwise there would be no sacred scripture.

The Fear, Love, and Knowledge of God

With both these principles in mind, namely, the primacy of silence and the power of language to express supernal realities, I wish now to say a few words about God from the metaphysical and spiritual points of view. I do so not only from the context of my own tradition, Islam, but also from what I have learned through personal spiritual experience and from what I have studied in the metaphysics and theology of both Islam and many other religious sources. Furthermore, I need to emphasize that the experience of the divine reality that we discern in many parts of the human family is not affected by time but transcends temporality. It is therefore a living reality today, as it was yesterday, and it is the heritage of all humanity, of all those who respond to the call of the Spirit, to whatever branch of the human family they may belong.

Let me begin with the basic distinction made in Islam between three modes as well as stages of approach to God, namely, fear, love, and knowledge of him. Our human relation to God falls under these categories; they also constitute the stages that the person on the spiritual path must traverse to reach the supreme goal of proximity to the divine.

Fear and surrender

In the spiritual life of the individual the three categories of fear, love, and knowledge—to which classical Islamic texts refer as *al-makhāfah, al-maḥabbah* and *al-maʿrifah*—are to be seen under the aspects of both simultaneity and temporal succession. There is something in human beings that must fear God, but the fear of God is not the same negative emotion as the fear of his creatures. As the famous Islamic theologian and Sufi, al-Ghazzālī, has said, when we fear one of God's creatures, we run away from it, but when we fear God we run toward him. It is this reverential fear that is essential to the spiritual life. We find it often in the Bible and the Qur'an. The saying of St. Paul, "The fear of God is the beginning of wisdom," has its exact Islamic equivalent. Our egos must shrivel before the divine majesty, and something in us must contract and die before we can expand, spiritually speaking. It is this fear of God's majesty that expresses itself in religion as service to God, and the performance of actions pleasing to him. Since service is related to the plane of action, we may associate it with reverential fear.

The attitude of service in this sense is closely related to that of surrender. God has given us free will; surrender means submitting our will to his will freely and not by coercion. This is a difficult surrender, and yet, when one succeeds, so sweet. There is a moment when we will all have to surrender to God—the moment of death that is beyond our will. Blessed are those who can experience that moment now through the exercise of free will rather than by necessity. This is the secret of the saying of the Prophet of Islam, "Die before you die," to which the Sufis add, "so that you will not die when the moment of ordinary death arrives." It is interesting to note that the German mystical poet Angelus Silesius, whom some authorities such as A. M. Schimmel believe was influenced by Sufism, expressed the same idea in almost the same words. The "dying before one dies" refers to spiritual or initiatic death through perfect surrender to the divine will, an idea we find also in other mystical traditions such as those of Christianity, Judaism, and Hinduism and, *mutatis mutandis*, even in a non-theistic tradition such as Buddhism.

To be able to surrender one's will to God turns even trials and tribulations of life into sweet victory. It is, however, very difficult to achieve, because God has given us freedom and wants us to surrender our wills to him both through fear of him and love for him. This existential situation in which we find ourselves demonstrates the grandeur of the human state and the consequence of our being created in "his image." We share in some way in both God's necessity and freedom. Surrender means giving up this relative freedom before that absolute necessity that is God.

In Arabic the very word Islam means both surrender and the peace that issues from it. All other creatures are in a sense *muslim*, since by their nature they are "surrendered" to him and cannot rebel because they have no free will. In the context of the Qur'anic revelation, the word *islām* is used not only in the sense of the religion brought by the Prophet or the surrender of all creatures to God. It also means surrender to God within any religious context in general. That is why the Qur'an specifically calls Abraham, the father of Semitic monotheism, "Muslim." In that sense *islām* is the generic term for all authentic religion, whatever its formal structure might be. From another point of view it can be said that there are three levels of meaning to the term *muslim*: the first refers to all creatures, save the human, which are by nature surrendered to God; the second to those who have accepted the Qur'anic revelation and are called *muslim* in the ordinary sense of the word; and the third to the saints who are in perfect surrender to God, and who are therefore the complement of the cosmic order, except that their surrender is conscious while those of other creatures is by nature and constraint. Surrender on the part of the human being is significant precisely because of the gift of free will, the element within the soul that makes possible the committing of acts of evil as well as acts of goodness.

Love

Surrender to God is also related to love, which follows the fear of God and which, along with knowledge, is the grand path for spiritual realization. Many Western authors have written over the centuries that Islam is based only on a conception of God as judge and has no understanding of the love of God. That is why in the past so many in the West who studied Sufism and discovered its great emphasis upon the love of God concluded that Sufism must have come from a non-Islamic source. They had perhaps forgotten that one of God's ninety-nine sacred names is *al-Wudūd*, meaning "Love." The Prophet of Islam was also called *Ḥabīb*, meaning "lover"; and Sufi poets such as Rumī and Ḥāfiẓ often refer to God as the Beloved. Moreover, a saint in Islam is called *walī Allāh*, literally the friend of God, or sometimes *'ashiq*, meaning lover of God. All of these terms are common in everyday Islamic parlance.

In any case, in Islamic spirituality there is no possibility of the love of God without an awareness of his majesty and transcendence, and without the fear and surrender that that transcendent and majestic reality requires of us. The love of God must be such that all other love is dissolved in it. The spiritual person cannot love anything outside divine love. For the spiritual person all love is a reflection of that ultimate love. Ultimately all love is God's love for his own theophany within us and within his creation. We are but the channels for that greatest love, which is God's love for what is ultimately nothing but himself.

Knowledge

Finally, there is the knowledge of God that is existentially based on both fear and love of him, although not dependent on these in its essence. To know God in a realized sense requires that we possess both fear and love combined with faith (*īmān*). From the human side, knowledge depends on the heart and intellect alone. It depends on the heart that is the instrument of *noesis*, and on intellection in its original sense of the divine realities. The light and grace that emanate from the divine and faith from the human side are also absolutely necessary for the attainment of realized knowledge. Unfortunately, contemporary linguistic usage has equated knowledge with only the conceptual, rational, and empirical. It is depleted of its sacred nature, so that there is much ambivalence about how we use it in relation to God. My Gifford Lectures, *Knowledge and the Sacred*, focused on the question of the resacralization of knowledge in the context of the contemporary West. In Islam, as in nearly all other religious traditions, the acquiring of knowledge is in itself a sacred activity. Knowledge is inseparable from the sacred. To know is ultimately to know God. The ground of the intellect is the divine; so is its ultimate goal. We can know nothing in essence without knowing the divine reality manifested in it. Traditionally speaking, all authentic knowledge leads to the knowledge of the one who is the end of all knowledge. This kind of knowledge is not conceptual knowledge, but what Islamic philosophers call knowledge by presence. It is not rationalistic knowledge, although reason itself is a ray of the divine intellect. It is ultimately knowledge by means of the divine spark within us, a spark that itself issues from the divine light. As in the case of love, so in the case of knowledge—and even more so—knowledge of God is in the deepest sense the knowledge *by* God of himself through us in whose heart he has placed the light of the divine intellect. That is why in Islam the "knower of God" or the gnostic in its original sense is called *al-'arif bi'Llāh,* the knower *by* God.

Before the secularization of knowledge in the West during the Renaissance and the 17th century and even before the rise of nominalism in the late Middle Ages, which marked the swan song of medieval Christian philosophy, the Christian wisdom mystics also held such a view. With Descartes, knowledge became bound to the radical separation or bifurcation of subject and object, and to the desacralization of both poles involved in the act of knowing. In the West today, whether one speaks of philosophy, science, anthropology, or even theology, one operates consciously or unconsciously within the framework of Cartesian bifurcation and therefore in the context of a desacralized conception of knowledge. But I am not speaking of this kind of knowledge in addressing the question of the knowledge of God. Knowledge transcends miraculously the dichotomy of subject and object. This kind of knowledge rests on the unity of knowledge and being, of the ultimately sacred subject and the ultimately sacred object. This unity is impossible to reach through mere conceptualization, which by definition rests on the mental concept imposed by the knower on the known.

The Oneness and Infinity of God

The hierarchy of fear and service, or of action, love, and knowledge of a metaphysical nature leads to a vision of the divine reality and allows us to make assertions about God that are nontemporal, but as true in the year 2000 as they were in 1000, and will be true a millennium from now. The first assertion that we can make about the divine is that the ultimate reality or God is one. This truth, emphasized so much by Judaism and Islam, may appear to some to be a pleonasm, an obvious fact not in need of being emphasized over and over again. But this assertion is more profound than simply to state that there is only one judge sitting on a throne in heaven rather than two. Such a meaning is certainly present, and on its own level is very important. It can prevent many a simple soul from falling into error. But there are many more profound levels of inner meaning in such an assertion.

Integration

Let us remember that oneness implies also integration. The word *tawḥīd* or oneness/unity that is the alpha and omega of Islam means at once the state of being one—with all the metaphysical meanings that that has above and beyond the numerical significances of oneness—and the act of making into one, or integration. The statement about the oneness of God is not only about God. It is also about the interrelation of all things and the integration of all things, including ourselves, into the center where the one God "resides." Without the oneness of the one who is the origin of creation, there would not exist that inner *sympatheia* between all things, the inner bond that binds us not only to God but also, by virtue of that relationship, to each other and to all of creation. That there is a *uni*verse is the result of the oneness of the divine principle, while all harmony in the universe in all its different levels is nothing but the reflection of unity in the domain of multiplicity. The oneness of God also means ultimately that there is but one being and that all existence issues forth from that original source.

The implication of God's oneness is also that we ourselves also have to be one. The fallen human species, removed from that primordial norm in which God created it, is like a house divided unto itself. As Christ has said, such a house cannot stand. Our acts do not arise from a single center or from harmony; nor are our minds in a ready state of concentration. Rather than being mindful and concentrated, we are usually scattered mentally as our emotions pull us in different directions. When we affirm the oneness of God, we do not immediately gain knowledge of what that oneness means, that *tawḥīd,* the highest meanings of which are known to God alone. But we do realize that we must lead an integrated life, rooted in a divine norm that makes possible the integration of our whole being, including our thoughts, emotions, and actions. This is the first major consequence of *tawḥīd.* The second is the realization of unity within all of creation and awareness of the interrelatedness of all that exists, from the lowly dust to the highest stars in heaven. The third and highest consequence is to realize that there is ultimately but a single reality, the gradations and manifestations of which constitute the realms of multiplicity.

All traditional cosmologies are based on the principle of the interrelation between all things and the dependence of all things on the One. The modern West has neglected this principle for several centuries, and only now is learning to speak of wholeness and integration. It is doing so because of the environmental catastrophes brought about by a segmented view of reality, dominant in the West since the Renaissance. Here in Oregon with its magnificent trees, the debate about whether to cut or preserve forests is taking place because for some forty thousand years before the coming of the white man, Native Americans lived in these forests with a religion and worldview that emphasized in the strongest terms the interrelation of all things and the sacred quality of nature. Had such a cosmology not existed, the trees would have been cut long ago and there would not even be a problem to debate today. In recent years integral studies and holistic philosophies have become popular in certain circles. Interest in such philosophies arises out of the need to rediscover the forgotten unity that encompasses all creatures and the unity that flows from what Islam calls *tawḥīd,* the principle central to its perspective. This doctrine, far from being a pleonasm, is cardinal in defining who we are, where we are, where we are going, and what our relation should be to other creatures while on our terrestrial journey. From *tawḥīd* flow consequences of the utmost importance for all people, whatever the age in which they live, and teachings that are especially pertinent in the present situation in which we find ourselves.

Some Christian theologians in their defense of the Trinity oppose the Jewish and Islamic emphasis upon unity, and some Muslims believe that Christian trinitarian doctrine is the negation of *tawḥīd.* Nevertheless, if we study the matter in its inner meaning and at greater depth, we will realize that, metaphysically speaking, the idea of Trinity does not negate that of unity. That is why for centuries Catholics have repeated in the Nicene Creed the phrase, "I believe in one God (*credo in unum deum*)." Whatever Muslims say of the oneness of the divine principle in Islam applies to other traditional and orthodox religions, even though some do not emphasize the doctrine of divine oneness as much as do Jews and Muslims.

God as Absolute, Infinite, and Good

In addition to being one—or, in Islam, *the* One, *al-Aḥad*—the divine reality also possesses other attributes about which one can speak in a positive manner. We can speak thus, provided that we preserve the symbolic quality of language—symbol being understood here in its traditional sense and not as sign or metaphor—and provided also that we do not reduce language to purely logical and operational definitions, as so much modern Anglo-Saxon philosophy does. First of all, God is absolute. This term is anathema in relativistic philosophies, which claim that there is no absolute and that everything is relative except this state-ment itself, which they then take to be absolute. But such criticisms are irrelevant from the point of view of traditional metaphysics, and I continue to use the term absolute according to the teachings of the perennial philosophy, to which I adhere philosophically.

God as pure actuality and All-Possibility

The God who spoke to Moses on Mount Sinai, who addressed Christ in the desert, and whom the Prophet of Islam encountered during his nocturnal ascent (al-mi'rāj) is absolute. Metaphysically, absoluteness in this highest sense means that God is completely and totally himself, excludes all that is other than himself, and bears no division within himself. There is nothing in God that is not completely "there" in the metaphysical sense. In the nontheistic world of Buddhism this quality of absoluteness corresponds to "suchness." Moreover, God is also infi-nite in the sense that everything that is possible is already contained in its essence in the divine reality.

There is a metaphysical question concerning the relation between potentiality and possibility, since both words come from the same Latin root, and since God is pure actuality, possessing no potentiality what-soever. Unfortunately, I cannot delve into this question here. For the purpose of the present discussion it is enough to state that while God is pure actuality from the point of view of being, he contains within himself the root of all things and is the treasury containing all the pos-sibilities that have been or will be manifested in the cosmos, to use the language of Islamic metaphysics. God is infinite and what we can call the All-Possibility. The doctrine of divine infinitude is an esoteric one, not usually discussed in ordinary theological texts, but it certainly exists in Western sources as well especially in the Kabbala and certain Christian mystics. Finally, God is the perfect good, as Plato would say, to' agathon, or perfection (kamāl) as we find in many Islamic sources. To know God is to know that he is absolute, infinite, and the perfect good, to use the formulation that goes back to Frithjof Schuon.

Masculine and feminine aspects of the divine

The first consequence of this knowledge is to realize that the distinctions between genders, far from being accidental, have their roots in the divine reality itself. The duality that manifests itself in masculine and feminine, in human, animal, and vegetative life and in other ways in the nonanimate world (including for example polarity in magnetism or positive and negative charges in electricity) has its roots in the divine nature. The masculine has its source in the divine as absolute and the feminine in the divine as infinite, which is also the interior and inward aspect of the divinity. It is interesting to note that while Islam regards God as the creator and revealer as having a masculine character, it sees the nonmanifesting aspect of the divinity as having a feminine character, the divine essence itself in Arabic being *al-Dhāt*, which is grammatically feminine. Also while the masculine aspect of the divinity is associated with justice, rigor, and majesty and is related to the divine name *al-Jalāl* or "majesty," the feminine aspect is associated with mercy and generosity and is related to the divine name, *al-Jamāl,* or "beauty." The name for divine mercy itself, *al-Raḥmah,* is in feminine form. Since Arabic is a language in which gender is clearly defined in both nouns and verbs, it is easy to see in the Qur'anic description of God at once the masculine and feminine dimensions of the divinity as well as the reality that the message of the Qur'an addresses both sexes and concerns them equally.

The absoluteness and infinitude of God also mean that on the one hand God excludes all otherness, all relativity, and all becoming and, on the other hand, that all creation is an externalization of realities whose metaphysical roots are in God. Creation is in the deepest sense the self-determination and self-manifestation of God. It is given to human beings, therefore, that they should live in such a way that they can at the same time be constantly aware of the reality of God as the absolute and of the evanescence and evaporation of all existence before that immutable reality. They should live in such a way that they are conscious of the truth that all things, to the degree that they exist, issue from God and have their roots deep in the Infinite. In fact, while God is absolutely beyond, all things are mysteriously hidden in the depths of God.

God as Good

As for perfection and goodness, Islam shares with Christianity and Judaism the cardinal idea that goodness in itself belongs to God alone and that all good comes from God. Only *the* good, that is God, is absolute goodness, for as Christ said, "No one is good but God alone." This also explains why there is evil in the world. Since the world is not God, it cannot be absolutely good, and this absence of goodness appears in the world of relativity as evil. Evil is the consequence of the existential separation from the source of all good, that is, *the* good as such. The answer to the question "Why should there even be a world?" lies in the infinitude of the divine nature, which by virtue of its infinity had to include all possibilities, including the possibility of the negation of itself, which is the world. Evil is the moral aspect of that separation from the source, which the world is by its nature. As Dante expressed it so beautifully in the *Divine Comedy*, evil is separation from God, and the pain of hell is precisely the awareness of this separation from the source of all beauty and goodness.

God Transcendent and Immanent

Two dimensions of God: transcendence and immanence

The attainment of sapience or gnosis (*ma'rifah*) also makes it possible to realize that God is at once transcendent and immanent, totally other and completely here. In the practical life of the spiritual seeker there is a pendular motion between the consciousness of these two relations that are ultimately one. However, in the context of the modern world, in which so many seek the divine as immanent while rejecting the transcendent, it is important to emphasize that there is no possibility of experiencing the immanent before surrendering oneself totally to the transcendent. The attempt to reach the divine immanence without recourse to the transcendent is one of the gravest errors of our times. Some, for example, think that they can reject traditional religions but through some form of self-realization become another St. Francis and see God everywhere. What a delusion—to look for the sun in the bottom of a well! One must first cast one's eyes to the heavens to behold the sun, or at least accept its reality and presence before being able to contemplate its reflection upon a lake. We must realize, to use the language of the Qur'an, that "there is nothing like unto him," and that "he is greater" than anything that can be said about him before we are able to realize that God is nearer to us than our jugular vein. The rhythm and pulse alternating between farness and nearness, transcendence and immanence govern the life of the spiritual person, but the metaphysical doctrine concerning God must of necessity include both dimensions.

In Islam it is not God who is veiled from us. It is we who are veiled from God. In a sense it is not God who is the mystery; it is we. If we could only lift the veil over our eyes and realize who we are, we would know God. That is why the Prophet said, "He who knows himself knows his Lord." There are many Arabic and Persian poems that rhapsodize about the mystery that while God is so close to us, we are so veiled and distant from him. In the deepest sense we are veiled from God precisely because of his proximity to us. Since he is everywhere, we cannot perceive his presence. If it were theoretically possible for him to be separated from the reality that we experience, we would be aware of that separation and absence. But until we have opened our spiritual eye, it is that ubiquitous presence that we interpret blindly as the "ordinary" existence that we equate with the absence of God.

God personal and impersonal

Also, God is at once personal and impersonal. Some Muslims do not wish to translate "*Allah*" as God for many reasons, including trinitarian associations with the term *God* as used in English. I am not one of them. There is nothing essentially privative in the term *God* (or, for that matter, *Dieu* in French or *Gott* in German), if we keep in mind its most universal and all-embracing meaning, including what

Meister Eckhart would call the *Gottheit* or the Godhead. In its most universal sense the term *God* in English is not bound completely to the trinitarian relationship that we find specifically in Christian theology, nor is it limited only to God's personal aspect. God is both personal and impersonal, as the name *Allah* signifies in Arabic. God has a face turned toward his creation and toward us, but that does not exhaust the divine reality. God loves his creation and we are able to address him in our prayers, but we can also contemplate him as an infinitely extended placid sea on which we fall gently as snowflakes, dissolving in that calm and peaceful water. God is the "thou" whom we address in our "I-ness," but he is also the infinite reality beyond all duality, impersonal while possessing the face turned toward creation that we experience as the divine personal reality.

This is the point at which the monotheistic conceptions of God meet the nonpersonal and nontheistic conceptions of the divinity in such religions as Confucianism, Taoism, and Buddhism, not to speak of Shintoism and the primal religions. In these religions there is certainly the sense of the sacred, the possibility of spiritual realization, religious ethics, and even prayer, but all within the context of the impersonal conception of the divine. The Buddha nature, just to speak of Buddhism, or the state of *nirvāna*, is the realization of the subjective pole of the impersonal divinity. To understand God as the personal as well as the impersonal is to reach a knowledge of the divinity that is all embracing and includes all different metaphysical and spiritual possibilities. To consider not only the face of God, to use the Qur'anic terminology, but also the infinite reality of the divine beyond the realm of being and "existentiation"[30] is to take nothing away from the glory of God. On the contrary it is to attest to the fullness of God's majestic reality.

God and Temporality

When we attempt to speak about the knowledge of God in the context of contemporary skepticism and the secularization of the knowledge of God, it is necessary to emphasize—and this is taken for granted in all traditional civilizations—that there is such a thing as the science of God, which is indeed the supreme science. The meaning of the term "theology," which originally meant such a science, has become so diluted in the West today that it is necessary to use another terminology to designate this highest of all sciences. I have tried to resuscitate the term *scientia sacra* in its Latin form in order to avoid the limitative connotations associated with the term *science*, especially in the English language as we use it today. I have even written a book entitled *The Need for a Sacred Science* with the aim of creating a consciousness of the importance of sacred science, the highest form of which is precisely *scientia sacra*, the science of God or of the ultimate reality.

Scientia sacra: the science of God

Since the Renaissance, metaphysics in its authentic sense became more or less forgotten and soon relegated to a branch of rationalistic philosophy. Gnosis in its turn has continued to possess a negative connotation, at least in the Western Christian milieu, as a result of its association with the historic Christian heresy of Gnosticism. In Eastern Christianity, in contrast, it remains a perfectly respectable and indeed central reality. A number of Catholic theologians such as Henri de Lubac and Hans Urs von Balthasar have tried to resuscitate its positive meaning, but the general anathema against it continues in many circles. That is why, while using both the terms *metaphysics* and *gnosis* in their original meaning, I find it necessary also to emphasize the term *scientia sacra*. In every integral traditional civilization there is something that corresponds to philosophy, something to theology, and something to what one can call metaphysics in its authentic sense, or gnosis, or theosophy. For example, in Islam one can observe clearly the presence of the schools of *falsafah* (philosophy), *kalām* (theology), and *ma'rifah / 'irfān* (gnosis). The latter category has been forgotten or at least eclipsed in the West, and it is precisely this category that concerns the science of God and what can be called *scientia sacra*.

In trying to approach God at the beginning of this new millennium, we must take this *scientia sacra* seriously again and turn to the task of resacralizing knowledge. Should we take this science of the real and place it once more at the center of our intellectual concerns, it would affect all realms of knowledge and let us see how to envisage knowledge and how to teach it formally in academic settings. Until that takes place, however, it is necessary to swim against the current and to point to the reality of this supreme science that, when realized fully, will transform us completely and lead to our spiritual salvation and freedom from the bondage of ignorance.

Historicism

Since we live in the world of change, it is also necessary to say something about the relation between God and the world of change and temporality. The spiritual person in quest of God today is not usually interested in developing a philosophy of history à la Hegel. Nevertheless, as a result of the historicism developed in the 18th and especially the 19th centuries in Europe and still dominating the current worldview of the West, many who enter the path leading to God are confused between the manifestations of God in the spatio-temporal domain of reality and the divine reality itself that transcends all becoming. God, while immutable, is also the source of all that changes; but the divine reality cannot be imprisoned in time. There is a tendency in the modern world to reduce everything to the historical and to reject as unreal everything that cannot be proven historically. This view of things constitutes the philosophical position called historicism, a most dangerous intellectual perversion that has done the greatest harm to religion in modern times. One can accept the significance of history without falling into the trap of historicism. For this reason I use when necessary the term *historial* as distinct from *historical*.

To accept historicism, either consciously or unconsciously, is to negate the permanent in favor of the transient. We see this clearly at a time when the transient has come to constitute almost the only reality and then comes to replace the permanent in our mind and thought. Many today worship "the times" as a divinity, even if they are not aware of it. Already the seventies are for many like the Pharaonic period. *Our* present moment in history is alone significant, but paradoxically our insistence on an extreme form of historicism has led to the destruction of history itself. Postmodern man has come to "absolutize the transient." We have come to take "our times" too seriously, losing our vision of the timeless and also the significance of our sacred history in which timeless values became manifest in the world of transience and impermanence. This attitude is a truly demonic perversion of the Sufi idea of being "the child of the moment" (*ibn al-waqt*), that is, living in the now, which is the sole gate of access to the eternal. The serious quest for God means taking a step away from this position that is based on a one-dimensional vision of reality. We must be able to remove ourselves from the stream of mere change and becoming, in order to be able to gain a vision of the immutable and the eternal in itself, and also to be able to contemplate the immutable archetypal realities in the world of becoming.

Even in traditional societies this need was present and came to different expressions in monasticism in Christianity and Buddhism, in becoming a person outside a caste or a *sannyāsin* in Hinduism, or in withdrawing inwardly from the world while living in it, as in Sufism and Jewish mysticism, religions that do not accept the formal institution of monasticism. How much more is that true for today's world when the world of transience has become so emptied of the sacred!

Seeing God everywhere

I must return to the question of the relation between God and the world of manifestation on one side and our approach to God on the other, as beings living in time. We must remember, immersed as we are in multiplicity, that we begin our journey as creatures possessing consciousness of things, objects, people, colors, forms, etc., around us. Spiritual growth means usually the step-by-step realization that all things come from God and return to God, and that all things manifest some aspect of the divine reality. I say "usually" because there are exceptional cases where, as if struck by lightning, one comes to understand all these truths in an instant and by the will of heaven. The "realized sage" sees God everywhere. Everything for him or her is a symbol of a higher reality. Such a person realizes that not only are sacred scriptures a divine revelation but so is nature itself, God's primordial revelation about which the Qur'an speaks so often. The Book of Genesis points to the same truth, if one understands it according to its inspired traditional commentaries. God not only revealed the Decalogue to Moses and the Qur'an to the Prophet; he also revealed nature. In the deepest sense religion is not only for us humans but also for the whole of creation. As the Qur'an asserts, everything prays to God and praises God, not we human beings alone. If we only had eyes we could detect the message of God on the face of all things. According to a *ḥadīth* (tradition) of the Prophet, "God has written the mark of beauty on all things." This saying is particularly important for the understanding of Islamic art; yet, it also pertains to the whole of cosmic reality. If we cannot see the marks of beauty on the faces of creatures, it is because our eyes have lost their original power of vision, which Adam, the primordial man, possessed in paradise.

Seeing God in religions other than our own

To see the manifestations of God everywhere imposes upon us two duties or responsibilities that are of particular significance in this day and age: First, to see the reality of God in religions other than our own and, second, to be fully aware of the manifestations of God's wisdom, power, and presence in the world of nature.

For millennia, human beings lived in a homogenous religious world of their own and did not have to delve into the reality of other religions. There were some exceptions, such as the encounter of Islam and Hinduism in India or of Judaism, Christianity, and Islam in Muslim Spain. Even in these cases, however, the truly spirited contacts and exchanges were among the few who belonged to the inner dimensions of their own tradition. Ordinary human beings are created to live within a single religion, just as they are conscious of living within a single solar system, even though there are other suns in the firmament. To live any traditional and divinely inspired religion fully is to have lived religion as such. The destruction of the homogeneity of religions in the modern world has created a new situation for those who are affected by its secularizing forces, and yet seek religious truth. A medieval Christian or Muslim did not have to be existentially concerned with the "other," even if the "other" lived next door. Before the modern era a Christian woman would not most likely have become influenced by religious life in Banaras, even if she traveled there as a young woman from Montana. A modern young woman who did, Diana Eck, is now professor of Hinduism at Harvard, and has written with empathy about that religion when she went to study in that holy city.

This new spiritual and psychological climate created by the advent of modernism is one with which we now have to contend, especially in the more modernized regions of the world. The challenge of penetrating seriously into other religious worlds—and not as a philologist, anthropologist, or historian—is the most exciting intellectual task of today, if we take it seriously and without loss to our religious moorings. It is "the only new thing under the sun" in our time. Although still on a limited and more esoteric level, the task has had historical precedence. To accept and respond to this challenge is to become aware of the ubiquitous nature of God's presence. It is to be able to see the other "faces of God" that he has turned to human communities other than our own, thereby enabling each religious tradition to provide the means for its members to realize the goal or *telos* for which we are created.

The sacred quality of nature

Our second duty or responsibility is to become fully aware of the presence of God in the nonhuman creation, that is, of the sacred quality of nature. It is manifestly obvious that if we do not radically change our current attitudes toward the natural world, nothing else in this world will matter in the long run, because we will not be around much longer to concern ourselves with any issue! We cannot resolve the environmental crisis by means of cosmetic actions. It requires a profound transformation of the modern understanding of what it is to be human, what the world of nature is and what rights we have over nature. It makes all the difference in the world whether we see the majestic redwoods of the western states, or for that matter, the still-pristine forests of the Amazon or Borneo, as sacred trusts that one must protect, or simply as mere commodities from which we can benefit economically. To look on the natural world and its riches as only economic resources is a formula for gradual suicide. The new century demands of us to reinterpret modern economics within the matrix of ethics and environmental considerations or else we will perish as a species.

Why have we come to such an unprecedented impasse? Many secondary reasons can be advanced, but the primary reason is that moderns have cut off the hands of God from nature, creating a science from which they exclude the divine presence in nature. There are of course human beings in the modernized world who still believe in God, but for the majority of them, their vision includes only God's relation to humanity and excludes other creatures. But God is not only "our" God or at best the God of the whole of humanity. He is God for the whole of creation. The mollusks crawling on the seabed, the birds flying in the air, and the smallest fish swimming in the water are also God's creatures. By what right then do we decimate and annihilate species every day?

The knowledge of God means an awareness of His presence in nature and brings about the awe and respect that we must exercise toward this presence. When St. Francis, now chosen as the patron saint of ecology, lived in Tuscany, he loved the birds and trees of his homeland, but the beautiful countryside of Tuscany was not in danger of destruction. Therefore when he addressed the world of nature, he did not have to apply his love and knowledge of the sacred presence in creation to the formulation of a living theology and philosophy of nature, according to which human beings should live. Today, however, those who speak of God, and at the same time have concern for humanity, must also address themselves to God's creation. It is necessary to protect nature not on the basis of mere sentimentality but on the firm ground of the knowledge of God both in himself and in his manifestations. This principal knowledge is not only the supreme goal of life but is extremely crucial to our very survival as human beings. We need to articulate a metaphysics of nature that becomes the framework and guide for our attitudes and actions toward other creatures.

Approaching God requires of us that we seek the light that both illuminates and enlivens: the sun that is the source of liberating knowledge and the warmth that is the love that flows throughout the universe and gives life to all things. This is the light that will allow us to see the divine presence everywhere and to hear the voice of the sacred not only in the *B Minor Mass* of Bach but also in the song of birds, the chant of whales, and the thunderous sound of storms.

To Know That God Is

At the highest level to know God means to realize that only God *is*. The testimony of faith in Islam is *Lā ilāha illa'Llāh*, meaning that there is no divinity but God. Each person understands this sacred assertion according to the level of his or her awareness and comprehension. But on the highest level it means that there *is* no reality but the divine reality. At the end of the road one realizes that we are not, the world is not; only God is, and other things are nothing but the manifestations of this one eternal reality.

A verse of the Qur'an (LVII; 3) states, "He [God] is the first and the last, the outward and the inward." This apparently enigmatic statement summarizes the whole truth about God and our relation to him, if we understand its meaning according to the inspired traditional commentaries. God is the first, or the alpha, which means that God is the origin of all things. We have all come from God. God is also the last, or the omega, and so he is our final end. Not only we human beings but all creatures also return to God. Whether we like it or not, we must return to God. Our choice, based on our free will, is how and in what condition we make this return journey. Rūmī says that since we have to make this return journey, why should we not walk on the path of God with a smile and in submission to him through the exercise of our free will, rather than being pulled along the path by our hair while we kick and scream? In any case, this name, [God as] the last, means that, whether we like it or not, our return is to God.

The spiritual life

God is the inward, the inner dimension from which all that is external issues forth. The spiritual life is nothing other than the life of inwardness. Those who live in the inward dimension of being are also able to see all things with the eye of inwardness and therefore see the inner, spiritual face of things rather than only their outward form. The real difficulty in the verse of the Qur'an cited above, however, is the assertion that God is also the outward. This truth is the most difficult to understand, for if God is the outward, why do we not see him with the outward eye in the same way we see each other? The truth of the matter, however, is that God is the light *with which* we see all things. How can we then ever expect to see with the eye the light that is itself the source of our vision? God as the outward is everywhere, but it needs the opening of the inner eye or the "eye of the heart," as the Sufis would say, to perceive this reality.

We live in a world bound by these four essential divine attributes: We come from God; we return to God; God resides inwardly at the center of our being; and the world itself is nothing but levels of divine presence that we can perceive only with the inward eye. Happy are those who realize this truth before the moment of death while still alive and in possession of the gift of free will. Such persons will not but seek to serve, to love, and to know God and, through the realization thus gained, be true lights to the world. They will be willing servants of both human beings and God's other creatures. They will be lovers of the good, the beautiful, and all of God's creation. They will be the locus of that unitive and illuminative knowledge of God that is the ultimate purpose of creation and the fountainhead of all wisdom.

Follow-up Questions

SHN = Seyyed Hossein Nasr   Q = Questioner   M = Moderator

M   Thank you, sir, for that eloquent, wide-sweeping, and very challenging address. I was struck by the similarity in our journeys. I majored in physics in college, then went to seminary, and then did a Ph.D. in the history and philosophy of science, as you did. We were only a few years apart at Harvard, and I have been looking for the bridge between science and religion and working in many of the same fields that you have. So it's thrilling for me to hear what you have to say.

SHN   Thank you. I know many people who are trying to do that. Some theologians advocate being serious theologians and try to be second-rate physicists, and some physicists have tried to become theologians and do their task. There are a large number of physicists who have a very serious interest in deep theological issues today both in America and in Europe. That's a very good sign, for they don't have an inferiority complex regarding modern science like some theologians who bend over backward seeking to placate whatever "ism" happens to be prevalent.

M   Let's begin with a fax from Chapel Hill, North Carolina. It says, "You are an elegant and compelling spokesman for Islam. But many Americans have a perception of Islamic religion and culture that is determined by political events since the 1970s. How can this too narrow and mostly negative perception of Islam be changed and people be brought together in greater understanding of one another?" I trust this conference is one step in that direction.

SHN   Let's hope so. The question is very much on target. It's a very great tragedy that not only is there ignorance about Islam, but deliberate ignorance in some circles, which is much worse. Ignorance can be forgiven. Someone living in the Midwest or the far west of the United States might not know anything about Islam and therefore might simply believe negative things written about Islam. But there is, unfortunately, a deliberate attempt by some people to continue the negative stereotypes. I have been at the forefront of interfaith discussions involving Islam for many years, and I'm always saddened by the negative stereotypes. There are many people of goodwill in Christian and Jewish communities who now extend their hands to Islam as one of the three great monotheistic religions. But there are others in the political realm who prefer to muddy the waters.

The reasons for this must be understood. Two are most important. A Western person usually has no preconceived notions about Taoism or Buddhism. Let's imagine that the daughter of a Swiss family tells her family that she wants to become a Buddhist. They might be a bit astounded. But if she wants to become a Muslim, that's a big family crisis. That's because for almost a thousand years, the formative years of European civilization, Europe and Europeans felt threatened by Islam. Muslims advanced as far as Poitiers in southern France in the 8th century, and the threat, from the European point of view, continued at least until the Ottoman Muslim siege of Vienna in the 1600s. "The Turk," the Muslim, was a threat. For Europeans, Islam was "the other," the only "other" they knew. That's very significant for the psychology of a culture. Islam, on the other hand, knew many "others," and not just Jews and Christians. Islam knew Hindu India, Confucian China, black Africa, and so forth. But for Europeans, Islam was "the other," and for centuries a very powerful "other" and enemy. This image still lingers in the minds of many, even though many parts of the Islamic world are so politically weak. And of course, this negative image of Islam has been exacerbated by the Arab-Israeli conflict in Palestine.

There is also a second reason, which is not completely negative. Namely, Islam is the first civilization in the second half
of the 20th century (and here I deliberately say civilization, not
religion) to try to reassert its identity rather than simply accom-
modating itself to dominant Western culture. (In the long run,
I think serious Christians in the West will also be drawn to do
this). The attempt to preserve the identity of Islamic civilization has led to some erratic movements, many ups and downs,
and some terrible things happening. It's easy to see why.
Imagine, for example, that Western Europe sought to reassert
its identity from a pre-secular age—it obviously would mean
a lot of ups and downs.

So, if you add together the centuries-old fear of Islam as
"the other" and the contemporary effort to affirm Islamic
identity and civilization, you can understand where the negative stereotypes of Islam come from. It's a difficult situation for
Muslims, but not impossible. As Diana Eck mentioned, there is
a rapidly growing Muslim population in the United States.
Through their presence and personal relationships with others
in the states, and through lectures and reading, these unfortu-
nate misunderstandings can be overcome. I see signs of improve-
ment in the last decade.

M We now have a call from Wisconsin.

Q Thank you for your presentation. I think you said that God is
the origin of all that exists in time. You also said that evil is separation from God. Does this mean that God caused the separation? If all things come from God, how do you explain the
Holocaust and other issues of theodicy?

SHN This is a very important philosophical question that everybody
who studies religions should pay attention to. I begin with an
observation that I make as a scholar, not as a theologian or
philosopher. I do not know a single thinker in the Asian land
mass who turned against God because he saw evil or suffer-

ing in the world. Though suffering is universal, suffering as a reason for rejecting God seems to be a specialty of post-medieval European civilization. Why is this? What happened so that the issue of theodicy—how could a good God create a world in which there is evil—became a reason for turning against God? This is a question that should be investigated. I think part of the reason is the humanization and absolutization of the human state.

From the metaphysical point of view, the problem is quite easy to explain. God is infinite. The infinite contains all possibilities, including the possibility of the negation of itself; otherwise it would not be infinite. And that possibility—because God is good and gives—must manifest itself, and that comes in the form of the world. The world is by definition a negation of God. I want to go back to the beautiful Kabbalistic symbol of the empty space created by God to allow the world to manifest itself. You cannot say "world" and not say "evil," because to do that is a blasphemy against God. A person can realize goodness in this world, can eradicate evil around himself or herself, and that's why we're here. But we cannot eradicate evil as such—that would mean to eradicate the world as such. We must always remember that only God is good. The question then comes back to, "Why did God create the world?"

M   I'm very sorry, but we must end here.

6 The God of All Faiths
Karen Armstrong

Karen Armstrong is a writer, lecturer, television broadcaster, columnist, and author of eleven books. Her best-known book is *A History of God: The 4000-Year Quest of Judaism, Christianity and Islam,* which was on *The New York Times* best-seller list for many months. She teaches at the Leo Baeck College for the Study of Judaism and the Training of Rabbis and Teachers in London. She is also a member of the Association of Muslim Social Sciences.

Earlier in her life she was a Roman Catholic nun for seven years. Educated at Oxford, she taught modern literature at the University of London. In 1982, she became a freelance writer and broadcaster. She produced a number of television programs on religious topics in England: a six-part series on the life and work of St. Paul, *Varieties of Religious Experience,* and *Tongues of Fire.* Her television work in the United States includes participating in Bill Moyers's series *Genesis: A Living Conversation.*

Her books include: *Through the Narrow Gate,* a best-seller in Britain; *Beginning the World; Tongues of Fire: An Anthology of Religious and Poetic Experience; The Gospel According to Women; Holy War: The Crusades and Their Impact on Today's World; The English Mystics of the Fourteenth Century; Muhammad: A Biography of the Prophet; A History of God (New York Times* best-seller); *Jerusalem: One City, Three Faiths;* and *The Battle for God.*

Armstrong describes herself as "a freelance monotheist." Long one of the foremost British commentators on religious affairs, she is well on her way to a similar status in the United States.

When I was about eight years old, I had to learn this definition of
God in the Roman Catholic catechism: "God is the Supreme Spirit,
who alone exists of himself and is infinite in all perfections." I must
confess that at eight this somewhat dry description did not do much
for me. This is the God of supernatural theism, delineated at this conference by Marcus Borg: a being rather like ourselves writ large, with
likes and dislikes similar to our own. This God of classical Western
theism is the first cause of all things, responsible in some sense for
everything that happens on earth. He is wholly powerful and wholly
compassionate—"infinite in all perfections." Even though this deity
often seemed remote and abstract, I really tried to make supernatural theism work, so much so that when I was seventeen I entered a
religious order of nuns. It seemed clear that if the claims of the
church were true, there was nothing more important in life than getting to know this God and giving my whole life to him. (This was
the early 1960s, and it never occurred to me that God could be anything but male.)

The God of Supernatural Theism

Yet even at this early stage, I had problems with the God of the
Roman Catholic catechism. Had modern science, as some claimed,
disproved God's existence? If God was omnipotent and entirely
benevolent, how had "he" allowed such atrocities as the Nazi
Holocaust? Was it reasonable to suppose that a God of love would
reveal himself only to a tiny proportion of the human race, leaving
millions of Buddhists, Hindus, Muslims, Jews, Sikhs, and Taoists outside his divine plan? As I reflected on these problems, God made less
and less rational sense. These doubts were corrosive. As a young nun
I was increasingly haunted by the suspicion that there might after all
be nothing out there. This was confirmed by the fact that I was
unable to pray, which, for a nun, was clearly something of a draw-
back. Every morning I would spend an hour on my knees trying to
meditate according to the method devised by the 16th-century

Catholic reformer Ignatius Loyola in his *Spiritual Exercises,* but I experienced only a vacuum, an emptiness, a stultifying boredom. I found, to my dismay, that even though I was able to concentrate with no difficulty on secular subjects, I could not keep my mind on God for five minutes. I was expecting an encounter with Something outside myself, and was uneasily aware that when I did experience some devotion, I had usually engineered it for myself. It was merely an aesthetic response to the beauty or music of the liturgy or to the emotional rhetoric of a skillful sermon. Increasingly, I felt a complete religious failure.

Failing to discover the sacred

This was nobody's fault. I was simply engaged in a spirituality that was wrong for me. Not all forms of prayer are right for everyone. You have to "shop around" to find a spirituality that speaks to your particular condition. Further, my approach was wrong. I was thinking about God and meditating upon Him, using the same type of logical, discursive reflection that I employed in my secular studies. But the Sacred cannot be apprehended in this way. We need a more intuitive, imaginative process, similar to that which opens up the truths of art. Rational analysis is indispensable for science, mathematics, or medicine, but it cannot help us to appreciate one of Beethoven's last quartets.

All the great masters of the spiritual life in all the major traditions insist that reason and logic alone cannot bring us to God. It was no wonder that God made so little rational sense to me, and not surprising that I failed to discover the Sacred in my logically organized meditations. But the nuns who were instructing me were not to blame for this. I have since learned that an inappropriate reliance upon reason alone has long been characteristic of Western theology and spirituality, especially since the scientific revolution of the 16th and 17th centuries. Rationalism achieved such spectacular success that empirical reason came to be regarded as the only path to truth, and the more intuitive disciplines of mythology and mysticism were discredited. Western people started to think about God as an objective, empirical fact. This is the source of many of our current religious problems.

Even though nobody was to blame for my failure to find God in my convent, I thought that it was *my* fault. I had so many doubts, so obviously lacked the cast-iron certainty that, I assumed, characterized true faith. I knew that I was supposed to love God, but it was very hard to love a being who remained so determinedly absent. If I was really honest, I loved my parents or some of the other sisters far more than I loved God. Even the convent dog was more endearing than this elusive deity. At least the dog knew who I was and responded happily to my presence, whereas God seemed at best uninterested and at worst antagonistic toward me.

There were moments when, to be brutally frank, I wondered whether I even *liked* God very much. The God of supernatural theism often seemed to me like a cosmic Big Brother, a harsh taskmaster and overseer who recorded my every failing. In the convent, our superiors stood in the place of God for us, and we used to kneel down when they addressed us to remind us of that fact. Sadly, the God who was coming through to me in this way seemed a relentless nag, endlessly reprimanding me for my faults and obsessed with the minutiae of my behavior.

This was not an easy time to be a young religious. The reforms of the Second Vatican Council, which would later transform convent life, had not yet come into effect and our superiors spared no efforts to make us aware of our shortcomings. In retrospect, I am grateful to them. I was an oversensitive child and this abrasive treatment toughened me up in ways that I have since found useful. But at the time, the cumulative effect of this approach convinced me that religiously I was beyond hope. Why should God want to get in touch with somebody who, in her heart of hearts, did not even like him?

So with great regret, I left my convent after seven years as a nun, and for the next six years existed in a state of grief, which, I have since been told, is not uncommon after a departure from the religious life. I was anorexic and suicidal—not because I wanted to die, but simply because I did not know how to live. Gradually I recovered. I learned to make friends. They rescued me from this slough of despond and, as this happened, I felt my belief in God slip quietly away. He had never impinged much upon my life, even though, as I thought, I had given him every opportunity to do so. The doubts that I had tried to suppress in my convent came to the foreground of my consciousness and convinced me that the doctrines of religion were entirely constructed by human beings and, therefore, false. I assumed that I had finished with God and felt a great deal better for it.

Unanimity about the Ultimate

In the early 1980s, after a series of career disasters in the academic world, I found myself working in television. Because of my background, I was given the job of writing and presenting a number of religious programs for the new British Channel 4 Television, which took a rather iconoclastic line on faith. I embarked on these projects in a spirit of skepticism, determined to show that religion was simply not true. Yet gradually I found my attention caught by aspects of the spiritual life that were entirely unfamiliar to me. As part of my research for these programs, I found myself studying Judaism, Islam, and also Greek and Russian Orthodox Christianity, which we tend chauvinistically to ignore in the West, but which has a less rational and more mystical approach to the divine.

The study of these other faiths revealed that supernatural theism was a peculiar aberration of the West, which had taken firm root at the time of the scientific revolution. In all three monotheistic faiths, I found eminent theologians and contemplatives asserting that God was not *another* being, not even the Supreme Being. It was more accurate to say that God did not exist, because our notion of existence is too limited to apply to the divine, which represents another type of reality altogether. Some went so far as to call God "nothing," to remind us not to think about God as a personality like ourselves. All insisted that the reality that we call "God" is not accessible to logical thought alone. God can be discerned only by the intuitive disciplines of prayer, liturgy, contemplation, and ethical practice.

A universal search for meaning

I was astonished, as I studied, to discover the profound unanimity of the great religions about the Ultimate. I found this endorsing. Instead of seeing my tradition as a lonely, idiosyncratic quest, I now found that it was part of a universal search for meaning. Working in isolation from one another, and often in a state of deadly hostility, Jews, Christians, and Muslims had all been fundamentally at one about God.

At the very least, this seemed to tell us something important about the human condition. When men and women confront the Ultimate, they go through a remarkably similar mental scenario. A study of these other faiths showed me what my own Roman Catholic tradition had been trying to do at its best. (Even so, I have not felt any desire to return to the church.) Today I often call myself a "freelance monotheist." I see all three of these traditions as equally valid; none is superior to the others. Each has its special genius, each its peculiar flaws. I draw sustenance from all three. But even the label "monotheist" can be misleading. I have just completed a short biography of the Buddha, and have been enthralled by his insights. Monotheists have a great deal to learn from the nontheistic religions.

Religion natural to human beings

So what have I learned from my study of these different traditions? What teachings seem to be universally held by religious men and women? First: Religion is natural to human beings. Authoritarian priests and kings have not imposed it upon us. It is something that we have always done. We are creatures that constantly seek ecstasy, a word whose literal meaning is "a going beyond the self." It is one of the peculiarities of the human mind that it has experiences and conceives ideas that transcend it. In an ecstatic experience we feel most fully alive, lifted momentarily beyond ourselves and touched profoundly within. We feel in contact with the deeper dimensions of existence. Religion has been one of the chief outlets of transcendence, but there are others, and when people no longer find *ecstasis* in a synagogue, church, or mosque, they seek it in art, music, sex, or even, mistakenly, in drugs. When I said this recently in an American university, one of the professors told me afterwards that as far as he was concerned his chief ecstasy came from skiing: when he was so at one with his swift motion down the slope that he lost all awareness of his waking self and, when he reached the bottom, felt simply: "That's *it!*" There was nothing else to say.

Religion as an art form

This ecstasy is important because we are beings who fall very easily into despair. We are the only animals that have to live with knowledge of our mortality, and we find this vision of extinction hard to bear. It can make our lives seem meaningless and this can paralyze us. We are meaning-seeking creatures and, from the time we fell out of the trees and became recognizably human, we have created religions and works of art to convince ourselves that, despite the dispiriting evidence to the contrary—the natural disasters that slay the innocent with the guilty, human cruelty and injustice, the premature death of children—life has ultimate value and significance. Whereas dogs do not seem to agonize about the canine condition and find it easy to live up to their natures, we humans find it very hard to be humane. Reason alone cannot help us to cultivate this faith. Confronted with tragedy, we do not want a rational discourse, but may need to listen to music, read a poem, watch a sunset, or turn to prayer. Faced with the ineluctably painful facts of life, reason is silent and has nothing to say that can console us. That is why we should learn to see religion as an art form rather than as a statement of scientific and logically demonstrable fact.

A sacred dimension in human experience

I have also learned that when people have applied themselves seriously to the rites and disciplines of religion, they have discerned a
sacred dimension of existence. They have called this transcendence
"God," "Nirvana," or "Brahman." Monotheists say that this is a supernatural reality; Buddhists claim that it is entirely natural to men and
women. However we choose to interpret it, the Sacred has been a
universal fact of human life that transfigures our experience and gives
it meaning.

The traditions all insist that we can never define this transcendence.
It is ineffable and indescribable. It cannot be confined within any doctrinal system, however august. To explain or to rationalize our experience of the divine will kill it, just as heavy-handed literary criticism
can destroy the graceful eloquence of a poem. When we speak about
God or Nirvana, all the traditions assert, we are at the end of what
thoughts and words can do. God's existence cannot be proven. God is
not an unseen reality, like the atom, which we can establish by means
of mathematical and empirical experimentation, because God is
beyond the reach of the senses, as God is beyond all human categories.
But because men and women have learned to discern this sacred
dimension of existence, it is germane to our humanity and part of our
human experience.

The great traditions, I have also learned, tell us that while God cannot be reached by the logic of rational thought, the sense of the divine
has to be cultivated in rather the same way as we cultivate an aesthetic
sense. God is not a reality that we can experience as simply as we see
a book, a tree, or a table. We have to learn to look beneath the surface
of the mundane to glimpse this dimension, to see through the
unpromising outward shell to its sacred core. This requires practice. If
somebody who had never seen a single piece of Western art wandered
into a gallery in London or Washington, D.C., he would not be moved
by the paintings of Cezanne or Picasso. They would make no sense to
him. It is hard to listen to music of another culture, because we have

different expectations of melody and harmony. We know that we have to work at aesthetics. We have to educate our eyes and ears. Our appreciation grows in time; the depth of our insight into art, music, or literature will depend on our commitment, effort, and skill. A sense of the divine also takes time and requires hard work. Weighing up the evidence of God's existence in a rational way will not yield a sense of the Sacred; the myths and doctrines of any religious tradition only make sense in a context of prayer, liturgy, meditation, and ethical practice that trains and develops our capacity for an experience of God.

In Britain, only about six percent of the population attends a religious service on a regular basis (as compared to over sixty percent in the United States). People often say to me in Britain that institutional religion is entirely alien to them. They find the evidence for God's existence unconvincing, and—often with good reason—find church services uninspiring. They have not realized that the sense of God has to be developed with the same stringency and dedication as a gift for mathematics or playing the violin. It is no good expecting to see this sacred dimension with normal, mundane consciousness.

It is not surprising that British people, like other Europeans, have this inadequate view of religion, because the churches often give them a false impression and speak as though God were an obvious fact of life. In their theological writings and liturgical celebrations, they do little to evoke that sense of Sacredness. We should give as much care to our rituals as we would give to a Shakespearean production in a major theatre. If it is to move, exalt, inspire, and help people to look through the confusions of daily life to a deeper transcendence, liturgy requires more than mechanical or customary observance. It demands creativity, ingenuity, discipline, skill, trial, and sometimes error.

Transcending the Self

All the major traditions that I have studied teach that one of the essential prerequisites for true religious experience is that we abandon the egotism and selfishness that hold us back from the divine. They all teach in one way or another that we are most fully ourselves when we give ourselves away. It is ego that diminishes us, limits our vision, and is utterly incompatible with the Sacred. But it is very hard to rid ourselves of egotism. Much of what passes for religion is in fact an endorsement of the selfishness that we are supposed to transcend in the ecstasy of faith. People want their prayers answered; they want to "get to heaven." They go to church, synagogue, or mosque not to cultivate self-abandonment, but to affirm their identities. We get a "buzz" out of being right, and our religion can make us feel superior to others who have not "seen the light." Even when we are working hard to get rid of the ego, we can fall into a form of narcissism. Looking back, I can see that it is not surprising that I had no religious experience as a young nun. The excessive concentration on our performance, behavior, and motivation and the constant, scrupulous self-examination simply mired us in the egotism that we were supposed to transcend.

Egotism is so pervasive and ingrained that it is difficult to lay it aside. The religions insist in different ways, however, that until we do so we will not glimpse the divine but only a reflection of ourselves—a "god" in our own image and likeness. The grain of wheat, Christ said, has to fall into the ground and die, or it remains nothing more than a grain of wheat; if it dies, it bears much fruit.[31] Calvary shows how far self-abnegation might have to go before we can rise to a different mode of being human. The word *islam* means "surrender." One of the first things that the Prophet Muhammad made his converts do was to prostrate themselves several times a day in prayer. This was hard for the Arabs, who were averse to kingship and found it abhorrent to grovel on the ground like a slave. But the physical abasement taught them at a level deeper than the rational and cerebral to go beyond the limitations of the posturing ego, which is so protective of our pride, interests, identity, status, and survival.

When self-preservation and self-promotion are at the center of our lives or of our religion, our outlook is limited and we cannot see the infinite. We are confined within the prism of the ego and can only see things from our own point of view. Our vision of the world and of other people is distorted, because we only see how they will affect or advance or impede us. We cannot achieve the ecstasy, the transcendence of self, which gives us some apprehension of the Sacred. The struggle for survival in a flawed and cruel world means that egotism often seems endemic to the human condition. The religions offer a new way of being human. It is, they teach, selflessness that enables us to live in what Buddhists call Nirvana and what monotheists call the presence of God. But ego is not vanquished in a day, and so God seems elusive.

Ways of Approaching the Sacred: Theology

As a result of my studies, I have evolved two main ways of approaching the Sacred. The first of these is theology.

I still cannot pray in a conventional way. The memory of my dismal failure at meditation as a young nun is too painful and exhausting. But I have found that sitting at my desk, immersed in a sacred text or involved in the discourse of any one of the traditions I have mentioned, I have mini-seconds of transcendence, awe, and wonder that give me intimations of what an experience of the divine might be for more gifted souls. In London, I teach in a rabbinical college and my colleagues tell me that my spirituality is very Jewish. This is why Jews study Torah and Talmud. I have also found that St. Benedict instructed his monks to spend part of the day in *lectio divina* ("divine study"), during which they would experience moments of *oratio* or "prayer." Unwittingly, I seem to have stumbled upon a spiritual exercise that suits me better than the Ignatian meditation of my youth.

Theology as struggle

The study of theology will not work for everybody. We all have to find our own way. Today theology very often has a bad name. It seems dry, abstract, and boring. But theology should not be a loyal regurgitation of orthodoxy, requiring little thought or a mere juggling of acceptable ideas to produce a plausible answer to our current problems. When the Roman Catholic catechism had the temerity to ask, "What is God?", it assumed that it was possible simply to draw breath and define—a word that literally means "to set limits upon"—a reality that must go beyond all our thoughts and concepts.

The answers are not all in place. Each generation has to make the tradition speak to its peculiar circumstances and meet the demands of its unique modernity. We should not consult Scripture as though it were a holy encyclopedia where we can look up information about God and find instant solutions to our difficulties. If our liturgy demands the same creativity and commitment as a drama or a musical performance, theology requires the same effort as the composition of a poem. Like poetry, it is an attempt to express the inexpressible. It cannot be a dull statement of sacred fact, but should touch us as deeply as the words of a great poet, giving us similar intimations of ecstasy. Like all great art, theology should invade us and reach the core of our being. But like all art, it is what Muslims call a *jihad*, a word that should not be translated as "holy war," but rather means "struggle, effort." It is an attempt to find meaning against huge odds. As a theologian contemplates the 20th-century icons of evil—Auschwitz, Bosnia, or Rwanda—it is difficult not to fall into despair. Some of these catastrophes challenge the old certainties of supernatural theism. To find a facile "answer" to such enormities is bad theology. Often the theologian will have to admit that he or she cannot find a solution.

Theology as listening and attention

This is why I am not particularly disturbed by the atheism that has become so common in Europe. After the European experience of the 20th century—a century of genocide from start to finish—the old certainties of classical Western theism are no longer credible. Historically, atheism has always been a denial of a particular conception of God rather than a blanket refusal of the Sacred. Thus at an early stage of their history, Jews, Christians, and Muslims were all called atheists by their pagan contemporaries, not because they did not believe in God but because their notion of the divine was so different that it seemed blasphemous. Historically, atheism often marks a stage of transition, when the old theology no longer works and people are reaching for a new religious solution. Sometimes in a restaurant we eat a sorbet after a strongly flavored first course to cleanse our palates and enable us to taste what is to come. Today many people have to rinse their minds of much of the inadequate or lazy theology of the past.

This may mean a period of what mystics used to call the Cloud of Unknowing or the Dark Night of the Soul, while we wait for a new theology to emerge. This is where the connection between theology and poetry can be helpful. Poets tell us that they often have to "listen" for years while a poem rises gradually from the unconscious, line by line, phrase by phrase, image by image. The British poet John Keats described this receptive state as a condition that he called "negative capability," meaning, "when a man is capable of being in uncertainties, mysteries, doubts, without any irritable reaching after fact and reason."[32] Like a poet, many of us today must hold ourselves in the same attitude of silent attention. Keats also called this state a great darkness, in which one sees only particles of light. The Greek Orthodox theologians loved the image of Moses on Mount Sinai, which was enveloped in thick cloud when God descended to speak to him there. He could not see anything but he was in the place where God was.[33]

Ways of Approaching the Sacred: Compassion

Darkness can be bleak and frightening. Is there anything that we can do while we are waiting?

Here we come to my second way of approaching the reality of God. All the great world religions insist that the single test of any theology or spiritual practice is that it issues in practical compassion. This was the message of the great prophets of Israel, who declared that liturgical and ritual purity was worthless if Israelites did not care for the poor, the widows, and the orphans. The New Testament insists that a faith that can move mountains is useless if it is not accompanied by charity. The core message of the Koran is not a doctrine—the Koran is skeptical about theological speculation—but an assertion that it is wrong selfishly to build a private fortune, but good to share your wealth and create a just, decent society where vulnerable people are treated with absolute respect and equity. This is the test of any theology, any idea of God. It is not true that any doctrine about God is acceptable. If your vision of God makes you kind, patient, and selfless, it is good theology. If it makes you bigoted, self-righteous, unkind, or dismissive of others, it is bad theology.

Compassion, creative of a sense of God

I have come to believe that the practice of compassion is more than a test of faith. It is itself creative of a sense of God. The Buddha, for example, used to urge monks and layfolk alike to sit quietly and radiate feelings of benevolence, sympathy, and compassion to all four corners of the world. They were not to exclude—and this is the point—a single creature from this radius of love.[34] By doing this, the Buddha insisted, a man or woman would come to know *ceto-vimutti* (release of the mind), a phrase that in the Buddhist scriptures is a synonym for the attainment of the supreme enlightenment, and Nirvana, a state that is, perhaps, the Buddhist equivalent of God. Why was this? A habit of universal compassion breaks down the carapace of selfishness that holds us back from our best selves and the experience of the Sacred. It dethrones ego from the center of our lives and puts others there. It gives us an ecstasy that transcends the limitations of our mundane existence and gives us intimations of the boundless dimension of Nirvana. As an early Buddhist poem puts it:

> May our loving thoughts fill the whole world, above, below,
> across—without limit; a boundless goodwill towards the whole
> world, unrestricted, free of hatred and enmity.[35]

The practice of such benevolence liberates us from personal likes and dislikes, does not permit us to indulge the selfishness of antipathy, and prevents us from seeing others from a point of view of self-interest. It is a victory over the ego, and brings us into what monotheists call the presence of God.

The Golden Rule

A key text for me is the Golden Rule of Rabbi Hillel, an older contemporary of Jesus. A pagan told Hillel that he would convert to Judaism if the rabbi could sum up the whole of Jewish teaching while he stood on one leg. Hillel stood on one leg and said: "Do not do unto others as you would not have done unto you. That is the Torah. The rest is commentary. Go and learn it."[36] This is an extraordinary statement. There is no mention of God, Mount Sinai, the Law, the Holy Land—all values that are inseparable from mainstream Judaism. But I believe that God is at the heart of the Golden Rule. At times we are tempted to say something unpleasant about a colleague, a rival institution or religion, or another race. But if we ask ourselves on such occasions how we should like such a thing said about ourselves and then refrain from the remark, we would for that moment have transcended the frightened egotism that often needs to wound or destroy others to enhance our sense of self-worth. Living in such a way on a daily, hourly basis, we should, I am convinced, achieve the constant ecstasy that does not consist of exotic, alternative states of consciousness but brings us rather into the divine presence. As the late Jewish scholar Abraham Joshua Heschel once said, when we put ourselves at the opposite pole of the ego, we are in the place where God is.[37]

I may not be able to pray or talk to God, but I have found that trying to live according to the Golden Rule has brought me a measure of the *ceto-vimutti* of which the Buddha spoke. It brings about a liberation of sorts. During my years of despair after leaving the convent, several people told me how rare it was for me to say anything nice about anybody else. One person once told me that she would hate to be my enemy. I have a naturally sharp tongue, and in those days I used it to defend, as I thought, a crumbling identity, lashing out at others like a wounded animal. The practice of the Golden Rule helps to allay these fears and brings with it a measure of peace. I am certain that while waiting in the Cloud of Unknowing, like Moses on the mountain, we are in the place where God is if we learn to honor the Sacred in others and to give ourselves away. I have a favorite mantra, a couplet from the late British poet W. H. Auden:

> If equal affection cannot be
> Let the more loving one be me.[38]

The Buddha, who was averse to metaphysical speculation, used to say that if we learned to live for others in this way, whatever our fate in the next life, we would be happier in this one.[39] We certainly would not need to agonize about abstruse definitions of God, because, if we managed to perfect the Golden Rule, we would be living in a sacred dimension, even if we could not define it or prove it logically.

The Divine Enshrined in Every Human Being

All the world faiths, in their different ways, teach us that the divine is not simply something "out there," it is enshrined within every single human being.

Abraham

This is an insight found in one of the earliest passages of the Bible. Jews, Christians, and Muslims all revere Abraham as the father of faith *par excellence,* but from the Bible account it is very difficult to see what Abraham actually believed. He seemed to have little of the certainty that we associate with faith today. He is constantly in the dark, asking God questions, and getting remarkably unsatisfactory answers. On one occasion, he fell into a trance, and a horror descended upon him when he foresaw the fate of his descendants in Egypt.

Abraham did have one marvelous religious experience.[40] He was sitting outside his tent at Mamre in Hebron in the hottest period of the day, when he saw three strangers on the horizon. Strangers in the ancient

Middle East, as in our own time, were potentially lethal people. Very few of us would bring three total strangers off the street into our own home. But that is what Abraham did. He did not simply give them a sandwich and a glass of water, but prepared an elaborate meal for them, pouring out on these three total strangers, who did not belong to his ethnic or religious group, all the comfort and consolation that he could to refresh them during their journey. In the course of the ensuing conversation, it transpires quite naturally, without any great fanfare, that one of these strangers was Abraham's God. The act of practical compassion had led to a divine encounter. It had created a theophany, a revelation of the Sacred.

Loving the stranger

It is of the utmost importance that the recipients of Abraham's kindness were strangers. In Hebrew, the word for "holy" is *qaddosh,* which means "separate, other." A meeting with a stranger, who belongs to another nation or another race—who may even belong to a people with whom we are at war—can shake us out of our complacency. The shock of strangeness, the puzzlement, the initial, instinctive repulsion, can give us intimations of the otherness or holiness that is God. Our religious traditions should not encase us in a ghetto of righteousness, excluding and even reviling those outside. They should lead us to honor the stranger and love him as ourselves, dethroning the ego and placing the other in the center of our lives. I should like to end with a poem by my fellow countryman and fellow Londoner William Blake, which is called "The Divine Image":

To Mercy, Pity, Peace and Love
All pray in their distress;
And to these virtues of delight
Return their thankfulness.

For Mercy, Pity, Peace and Love
Is God, our father dear,
And Mercy, Pity, Peace and Love
Is Man, his child and care.

For Mercy has a human heart,
Pity a human face,
And Love, the human form divine,
And Peace, the human dress.

Then every man, of every clime,
That prays in his distress,
Prays to the human form divine,
Love, Mercy, Pity, Peace.

And all must love the human form,
In heathen, Turk, or Jew;
Where Mercy, Love and Pity dwell
There God is dwelling too.

Follow-up Questions

KA = Karen Armstrong Q = Questioner M = Moderator

M You spoke of the two spiritual practices of theology and compassion. Are there any others in your life?

KA I am not able at the moment to pray. I have such bad memories of all those years when I tried and failed. I feel exhausted and tired at the thought of speaking to God. That may change because my life has changed so much. I never thought at one time I would be ever thinking about God—and look at what happened. I don't recommend the position of a freelance monotheist, because I lack a community. I must say, though, that when I travel around the world as I do, I do find a community of like-minded people such as you. This is a weakness in my position, because community is of immense importance in the pursuit of God. I also don't have liturgy, and this isn't ideal either. Just because I am a monotheist today doesn't mean that I won't be something else tomorrow. I was, after all, an atheist before. In the quest one is always seeking, always changing, always moving on. If you are studying all day long, as I am, and getting involved in this compassion business—this is a full-time job. [*Laughter and applause*]

Q I find I have to pull back from organized religion. The thing that brought me here is my inability to pray. It was always very easy for me. I came to see public prayer as something for show. I saw that in my church, and started to see that in myself. So I have pulled back and am not in any community either. As far as talking to God is concerned, I have always done that. Now I wonder what place prayer has in my faith.

KA That's a very good question because it is not easy to answer. The fact that I do not pray does not mean that I do not recognize there is a place for prayer. There are difficulties, even theological difficulties, with prayer. Does God really need reminding that we are miserable sinners, and that he created the world? There is also the difficulty for me of the divine throwing us into vast buildings and making us sing his praises once a week. That has some unpleasant overtones for me.

One of the problems is that in the West we have made our prayers too talky. In *A Passage to India* Mrs. Moore is sitting in the cave and experiencing the emptiness and desolation that fills us all from time to time. Nothing in her British background helps her. She talks about "poor little talkative Christianity." When I was in the convent I experienced Roman Catholic liturgy in a very beautiful way. It was theater. And theater is not just for show. Theater began in the West as part of a religious celebration. It is a transcendent experience. It lifts you up out of yourself. It gives you *ecstasis*. But we have got into the habit of telling God things all the time. There is no time for silence or the silence that comes with liturgy.

The way to look at it is to understand that prayer is for us. God doesn't need us to be telling him how marvelous he is all the time. Liturgy is part of our battle against ego. It is teaching us to use language in a different way. We often use language to defend ourselves. It is automatic for us, for example, if someone accuses us of something, to say "Oh, I didn't do it" or "Yes, I admit it. But X, Y and Z were involved too." We very seldom admit the offense with our whole heart. (We very rarely thank with our whole heart either.) Life is tough out there. We can't be seen to be weak and relying on other people. Prayer teaches us to use language in a different way: to praise unreservedly, to thank unreservedly, and thus to lower the cautionary barricades we have erected around our fragile ego. That will let the sacred in. To regard prayer as something for us—that will let us experience the quietness of the divine. But I am not a good person to say this, because I am not praying myself. Perhaps I should.

It does help to have a program because prayer is so difficult. But you don't have to use the *Spiritual Exercises,* as I did when I was young. If you don't find the program you are using helpful, give it up.

Q   Can you tell us some of the questions you hope this generation will ask?

KA   One question I would like them to ask is, "What is religion for?" It isn't just to inflate us, or prop us up, or give us a security blanket. It is to help us to surrender ourselves to something greater. I hope also people will ask questions about human cruelty and the dreadful lessons we learned in the 20th century of man's inhumanity to man. Auschwitz can be seen as a dark epiphany. In an uncanny way Auschwitz reproduced the imagery of hell or inferno that had haunted Europe for centuries—the whips, the darkness, the flames, the stinking air, the jeering, the cursing. Hell has nothing theologically to do with burning pits. In Catholic theology it is the absence of God. When you look at Auschwitz you see the danger of human life when all sense of sacredness is lost. [*Applause*]

How do we recover a sense of the sacred regarding the environment, or the world that we have ransacked, or other human beings? That is what religion is for. There was a debate in London some years ago about whether women should be ordained in the Church of England. The former bishop of Durham, who was in favor of it, said, his voice trembling with tears, "This is a shame to us, that in a world that is crying out in its lostness, we are quarreling about gender issues instead of opening our hearts and bringing sacred compassion back into a world that has lost it."

Q   You mentioned that people seek ecstasy in a variety of ways other than through religion, such as art and sex. Can people's desire for spirituality be satisfied other than through religious means?

KA   Yes, but as with an important proviso. Religion has always used art. Drugs, no. Drugs are false ecstasy. I also have my doubts about skiing! [*Laughter*] Many people in my country have no sense of the very word "God." You would never fill a hall like this in London. But they are passionate for something. Art is one way by which people learn to look and listen, to see "eternity in a grain of sand," or to see the boots that Van Gogh painted as an epiphany, something brimful of meaning. But it must all find expression in acts of compassion. You can't just retire into a wonderful art gallery—to what Tennyson called "a palace of art"—and shut the world out.

Art can lead us to this attitude of awe and wonder. But there are dangers. Art can degenerate into pure self-indulgence. In London the death of Princess Diana was a truly religious event. It was extraordinary because we British are so reserved and cold. We don't weep in the streets. But London became like India. There was a smell everywhere of rotting vegetation from the flowers that people banked up in Kensington Gardens. Shrines appeared all over London. People were sitting under trees lighting candles. Why? Because in this girl, flawed as she undoubtedly was, they saw something of compassion. She was one who had suffered and tried to use her suffering creatively to reach out to others. In a depersonalized world she became for a moment a sort of goddess. All that can become self-indulgent, of course, and people can luxuriate in just the feeling, so it has to have a control. It has to be channeled into some kind of practical ethical activity.

I know the phrase "liberal humanism" is unpopular in conservative religious circles in the United States, but (and here I am indebted to Wilfred Cantwell Smith) it is a kind of religion with its own disciplines of mind and heart if it is observed seriously. There are many avenues to the sacred. If people are nauseated by the idea of God, and God becomes a block on the way to the sacred, then travel in another direction. You can go there by another route. Writing books, as I do, is a secular activity in some respects; but you can make it into a sacred one. People who paint, or write or perform music, or dance are in some sense involved in sacredness and giving other people intimations of sacredness. There are all kinds of avenues to God.

Q   What do you say to someone who, in a personal journey of discovery, comes to the conclusion that there is nothing out there but the void? Even the title of this conference implies that there is something out there—"God at 2000," as if to say, "How is the good old boy at 2000?"

KA   Theologians constantly point out that God is not a being, not even the supreme being. God is not one of the things that exist. Our notion of existence is so limited that it can be inaccurate to apply it to God. Some people therefore prefer to call God nothing rather than something. Maimonides developed a kind of exercise in which one says, "God exists." You listen hard to that. But you realize that is not right. So then you say, "God does not exist." And you realize that is not right either. So you say, "God does not not exist." It is not just a conundrum. It is a discipline that helps you understand that when we are speaking about God, we are at the end of what thoughts and words can usefully do. There has been so much inadequate theology around: "How is the good old boy at 2000?" is that kind of lazy theology. It is facile. People need to rinse their minds of it.

Sometimes people will say, and with great reverence, "Rather than think of God in an inadequate way, I will say there is nothing, no God." Scientists bring us face to face with the dark world of created reality where, it seems, there is nothing and no God. And yet, if people live with compassion and respect for this world, they will get intimations of transcendence. They will, even if they do not fasten these intimations onto a notion of a supreme being called God. The Buddha was as strict as any modern logical positivist in saying that language is not adequate to describe the divine. You cannot, he said, talk about an ultimate principle of being. But Buddhism has such profound respect for compassion. We have to get rid of the idea of God as the Big Brother, or the being that runs the world who sits up there in heaven, listening to our praises. To dismiss an idea of God like this can be a good and positive step. Without a strong sense of sacredness you fall into the kind of despair that I knew when I left the religious life and gave up the quest for the sacred.

Q   Your new book is subtitled, "Fundamentalism in Christianity, Judaism, and Islam." Do you have any suggestions for how to begin and sustain a dialogue with individuals who are fundamentalist and exclusivist in their beliefs?

KA   This is a huge question. It is essential to address it because we are in a world where nations are divided down the middle on the question. Fundamentalism is largely inspired by immense fear or a huge dread. Modernity for me has been wonderful and liberating. I can't imagine being a woman in any century but our own. But modernity is still scary. Some people gaze at it with dread, real dread, visceral horror. They gaze at a world that is desacralized. In the United States the belief in an imminent Armageddon with Jesus returning in glory—premillennialism— has a crazy mythology. But to laugh at it and dismiss it is not right. If people brought such fantasies or dreams to a therapist it would be a symptom of profound disturbance.

The fact that people are evolving such fantasies shows a huge malaise in modern society. When people are frightened in that way they become aggressive. Every single movement that I have studied in Judaism, Christianity, and Islam is convinced that the liberal, secular society is going to wipe them out. They have fears of annihilation. Just to say that these people are crazy is not helpful. Ignoring or ridiculing it is not the way to deal with it. Vilifying it makes it worse. When we are frightened or frozen in terror and people yell at us or laugh at us, it makes us worse.

What happened in the United States after the famous Scopes trial in 1925—when the fundamentalists tried to get the teaching of evolution banned in the schools—gave the secular press a field day. It poured utter scorn on the fundamentalists and ridiculed and laughed at them. As a result these people became more extreme. Up until the Scopes trial they had not been entirely literalist in their biblical interpretation. After the trial they became rabidly literalist. Before the trial some of them had been on the left of the political spectrum. Afterwards, they swung to the far right.

You can push people into a more extreme position. It is hard to open dialogue with people who tell you that you are diabolic or evil. That is why Jesus talked about turning the other cheek. We all have to listen to the suffering of others. We have to listen to these fears and learn to read the fundamentalist imagery of dread, fear, pain, malaise, or disassociation and listen to what all these represent. Then with compassion we can try to reach out to them. Whether we are liberal religious people or not, compassion is crucial. The same is true if we are secularists. Compassion or tolerance does not mean putting up only with congenial opinions. It means putting up with things we find viscerally awful. We have got to start talking to one another.

I have focused on fundamentalism in the United States. The same thing is true when you look at Judaism and Islam. The dread is there too. The fantasies about annihilation are not entirely misplaced because of the speed of modernization in Muslim countries, for example. Secularism for us evolved gradually over three or four centuries in a positive way. It has been imposed far too fast and too quickly elsewhere, and it is experienced as an assault. Atatürk closed all the madrasahs and Qur'an schools of education. He closed down the Sufi orders and forced people to wear Western-style dress. Forcing people into a secular society is going to make people feel that Islam is going to be destroyed.

These fears are not entirely paranoid fantasies. Modernity has gathered around itself all kinds of difficulties. The way that fundamentalists organize their society, the options or lifestyles they choose or create for themselves and the belief patterns that they build up all represent a mirror image—a distorted mirror image—of modernity. One of the hallmarks of modernity has been the emancipation of women. Hence fundamentalists in their reaction tend to overstress the traditional role of women. There are many flaws in the modern experience itself. Modernity is not benign to everyone. By studying how fundamentalists deal with it we can see some of its darker aspects.

Q   Dr. Borg has said something about the fact that we did not choose where or to whom we were going to be born. People are born French, Italian, or Spanish by accident. Maybe we are born into our religions by accident as well. Is there something in our present and future that will lead finally to there being no reason for conflict or disparagement among the religions because we all believe in one God?

KA That would be wonderful! It is a vision of Utopia and something we all long for. But believing in the one God does not do much for you unless you are also living your belief. That involves a huge compassionate offensive. Compassion is an unpopular virtue. We have got to keep trying. [*Applause*]

7

The Prodigal God
Archbishop Desmond Tutu

Desmond Tutu is among the best known and most honored people in the world today. As a priest, dean, bishop, and archbishop of the Anglican Church in South Africa, he was a leading figure in the struggle against apartheid. For his passionate advocacy of nonviolent change, he was awarded the Nobel Peace Prize in 1985. After apartheid ended, he was chosen by South African President Nelson Mandela to chair South Africa's Truth and Reconciliation Commission to investigate crimes committed during the apartheid era. In 1996, President Mandela presented Tutu with the first "Order for Meritorious Service" award, South Africa's highest civilian award. In 1998 French President Jacques Chirac presented him with the Legion of Honor, France's highest civil award.

Tutu is the author or editor of many books. They include: *Crying in the Wilderness: The Struggle for Justice in South Africa; Hope and Suffering: Sermons and Speeches; The Rainbow People of God: The Making of a Peaceful Revolution; The African Prayer Book* (ed.); *The Words of Desmond Tutu;* and *No Future Without Forgiveness.*

Tutu was born in the Transvaal area of South Africa. His father was a teacher, and Tutu himself became a high school teacher for three years. In his late twenties he began to study for the priesthood in the Anglican church, was ordained in 1960, and did three years of graduate theological studies in England. In 1975 he became the first black person to become dean of St. Mary's Anglican Cathedral in Johannesburg. In 1976, he became bishop of Lesotho. From 1979 to 1984, he was general secretary of the South African Council of Churches.

In 1984 he became the first black bishop of Johannesburg, and in 1986 he was elected the first black archbishop of Cape Town, and thus titular head of the Anglican Church in South Africa. He held this position until his retirement in 1996, when he became chair of the Truth and Reconciliation Commission. He returned to South Africa after completing a visiting professorship at Emory University in Atlanta, Georgia, in August 2000, and announced his retirement from public life.

My Personal Evolution

I have a collection of charming line drawings entitled "My God," by Mel Calman, the late cartoonist for *The Observer* newspaper in London. One shows God looking a little upset as God is bombarded with varied and often-contradictory requests from his human creatures on Earth. In some exasperation God mutters, "Sometimes I wish I could say 'Don't call me, I'll call you!'"

The cartoon I want to refer to shows God staring at a poster reading, "God is dead!" And God remarks, "That makes me feel insecure." For someone who was declared affected by rigor mortis and thoroughly moribund long ago, God does seem extraordinarily lively, refusing to let those so inclined to write his obituary. God could with justification say that reports of his demise were splendid examples of hyperbole. God does refuse to go away or to satisfy atheists and secularists by lying down quietly and not making such a thorough nuisance of himself.

God very much alive

The fact is that at the end of the second millennium, God has shown that he possesses extraordinary survival powers and resilience. Religion in some form or other, and belief in and worship of God, however conceived or described, are just facts of life, denied only by the willfully blind, the obtuse, or the perverse. *Newsweek* and *Time* magazines have run on a remarkably regular basis either major cover stories or substantial articles about God and the things of God. These two are hardnosed commercial enterprises depending on their ability to attract advertising revenue. Advertisers are not sentimental; they are interested in circulation figures. These magazines would not write on subjects of scant interest to their readership, either actual or potential.

In this country religion plays an enormous role, especially in public life. This observation is not a value judgment about whether that is or is not a good thing, nor is it saying anything about the nature of the religion that has had and continues to have such huge repercussions. My observation is merely phenomenological. It describes as dispassionately as possible the current landscape. It is a fact of life, and it sticks out like a sore thumb, for that influence has frequently been pernicious and baneful. We could say without fear of contradiction that anyone seeking public office who declared himself or herself to be an unbeliever or an atheist would have the same chances of election as a snowball to survive in hell. It is so much a part of the scheme of things that public officials take oaths of office almost always on a Bible. The assumption is that most candidates are not just believers, but Christians. Presidential candidates and those running for other offices spend considerable time wooing religious constituencies. For a long time there has been a fairly powerful group called the Moral Majority that clearly determined the fate of several candidates who had declared themselves on controversial issues such as school prayer, abortion, homosexuality, the death penalty, and so on. If these candidates did not toe what was frequently a very conservative line on those questions, then, as frequently, they knew they had no chance of election.

The face that religion frequently showed to the world at such times was not too pretty. It tended to be off-putting and in many respects it gave religion a bad name. That, however, is not the point we are making. All we want to establish as an undisputed given is that at the end of the 20th century and the beginning of the year 2000, God is very well, alive, and kicking.

In varying ways in western Europe it is also true that religion has revealed an extraordinary capacity to survive. In one Western country, the head of state is actually described as "Defender of the Faith." Religion is a significant factor in many Asian countries. One of the most serious problems in these countries is determining the place of minority faiths when the dominant religion is intolerant of rivals. Many scholars claim that the center of gravity of Christianity has shifted to Africa, and the largest Roman Catholic population is to be found in a Latin American country. In Africa and Latin America the aberration is to be a nonbeliever. As we survey the conflicts in Northern Ireland, the Middle East, Kosovo, Bosnia, Chechnya, Iraq, India, Pakistan, and elsewhere, conflicts exacerbated by religious differences, our cry should not be that there is little religion about, but rather that there is far too much religion abroad.

Yes, God is very much alive and kicking. But what kind of God?

A burdensome image of God

When my family and I first went to England in the early 1960s, I was invited on one occasion to a tea party. For some odd reason you were expected to pay for your own tea. I offered to pay for an English acquaintance I had met there. Now this person could well have responded perfectly understandably, "No, thank you!" You could have knocked me down with a feather when he retorted, "No, thanks. I won't be subsidized." Well, I never! Subsequently on reflection I realized that such a response, in many ways, was a prevalent attitude and it spilled over into our relationship with God.

Let me explain. That partygoer was really saying that he was not a failure. He could make his own way in the world. He could pay for his own tea. He reflected the current attitude that comes from the success ethic. To count in this world, you have to succeed. It does not much matter in the end how you succeed as long as you do succeed. Hence our adulation of the superstars or of those who have "made it." We set high store by competitiveness. We inculcate it at an early age in our children. They must not just do well in school, getting "A" grades or making the first team, and so on. They have to sweep the floor with their opponents. Our worth depends on our achievement or success. The worst thing that can happen to anyone is to fail. Then you are written off. Is it any wonder that stomach ulcers have become status symbols?

I think I accepted this way of looking at things. There is a legitimate place for effort, achievement, and success. I want to have the best surgeon operate on me, one who has worked hard and achieved distinction. But we have become quite obsessed with success, achievement, and the worth that we think these bring. For most of us this attitude has been transferred to describe our relationship with God. Most of us have believed that we needed to impress God. We had to succeed. We had to achieve or do good, in order that God should accept us, approve of us, and love us.

It all started with *us,* depended on *us.* God's attitude to us became a response to our achievements, success, or goodness. It was a reward for being good or virtuous. If we failed, then we were doomed. So we worked ourselves into a frazzle trying to impress God, seeking to make ourselves acceptable or lovable. That was the burdensome image that I had of God for a very long time. I thought that God was a kind of spoilsport, on the lookout to catch me out doing something wrong, or thinking or saying something wrong. God seemed ready to pounce and declare, gloatingly, "Gotcha!"

What a dreadful, life-denying deity! It was a total travesty of the wonder and glory of the true God. What a relief it was—no, a veritable liberation—when I learned that God is really the Prodigal God, incredible in the love that he has for all of us. It was tremendous stuff when I discovered the truth about the God of grace, the God and Father of Our Lord Jesus Christ.

Precious with a Worth that Cannot Be Compared

When I did find out this central truth about God—or did it find me?—it has since grasped me and possessed me, so that all my sermons and addresses are really about this one necessary fact. I have not yet worked out its full implications. I am still bowled over as the true significance of it unfolds day by day. It seems to have such enormous ramifications and implications. Perhaps, this side of death, I will never grasp comprehensively what it all means.

The one truth is this: God loves me. Full stop. The initiative belongs to God. It is not as if God were reacting or responding to something that existed before. No, the glory and the wonder, as St. John puts it, are not that we first loved God, but that God loved us first. Everything, just everything, flows from that fact.

I should have known this from the way the Bible has told the story of God. For there, in what should have been the paradigmatic account par excellence, we see God extraordinarily choosing not merely a people but a rabble of slaves to be God's own people. They had done nothing; they were nothing. They were not even a coherent group, but a troublesome, fractious, quarreling, complaining rabble of slaves. They were thoroughly insignificant, with nothing to commend them. They had neither earned nor deserved their election. Yet it is they whom God chose.

I should have known or been alerted to the nature of God and to the kind of relationship he wants to have with his creatures through reading the preface to the Decalogue. The preface declares, "I am the Lord thy God." Which God? "The One who has already delivered you out of bondage. Before giving you the law I have already acted in your favor, I have already chosen you before you had done anything to deserve being chosen."

As soon as we hear the words, "I am the Lord your God, who brought you out of the land of Egypt, out of the house of slavery" (Exod. 20:2), we should add the word *therefore*. "Therefore you shall not," and so on. The law is given *after* the Exodus has already occurred. Thus its observance could not have been the motive for the Exodus, since temporally it comes after. It was not given so that the Israelites could have something with which to impress God through their observance of it. The law was given to help this rabble of slaves become a people who could say "Thank you, God" in all aspects of their lives for the gratuitous act of deliverance and election. Instead, the people of the Exodus perverted the purpose of the law. They assumed their obedience to the law would impress God and make them acceptable, as if they had been chosen because somehow they were superior and deserved to be chosen. They did not want to be subsidized, not even by God.

But all along it was grace. It was a free gift bestowed prodigally and unstintingly by the God whose love was overflowing, generous, and infinite. They were forever in God's debt. Everything they were or possessed was given freely in overflowing measure by the God who is fullness of life and needs nothing outside God to be fully God.

I should have been alerted

I should have been alerted then that God's love bubbles over, that God was there from the beginning, fully and completely God in the vibrant life of the eternal Trinity. God did not need anything outside God to have fullness of divine life. Yet God brought creation into being because God *wanted* it all. It was all the consequence of God's love, the result of the outpouring of this divine love and life that have no beginning and no end. It was life from a life of eternal self-emptying, a divine *kenosis*. In the glory of the eternal Trinity, the outpouring of the divine love, God the Father pours forth, emptying all of the being of the Father into the Son, who, being coequal and coeternal, reciprocates in equal self-emptying measure, eternally bound in this act of mutual receiving and giving by the Holy Spirit. Forever pouring forth, forever self-emptying, forever receiving prodigally, generously, overflowingly: This is the only way God can be God.

Everything exists because it is loved and held in being, because it is loved by a love that is unchanging and unchangeable, and will not let us or anything go. Everything is a gift, prodigally and undeservedly given, to paraphrase Julian of Norwich in her *Revelations of the Divine Love*.

I should have been alerted to the nature of this God and to the kind of relationship he sought to develop with his creatures from the fact that he had chosen the undeserving, the repellent, the underdog, the downtrodden, the weak, and the powerless. God poured forth his bounty and graciousness without reserve and without measure. This is how God is in relation to God's creatures. Even whilst punishing Adam and Eve, God made skin aprons to cover their nakedness in place of their ineffectual covers. Even while driving Cain out as an outlaw, God put a mark on him so that none should kill him. God caused an ark to be built to save some of those whom his justice and righteousness had condemned, so that God's justice and wrath would be filtered and mediated only through love, mercy, and grace.

I should have been alerted to what kind of God this one was when he called Jeremiah to be a prophet and made the extraordinary assertion: "Before I formed you in the womb, I knew you." No one is ever an afterthought. We came into being because we were loved, and had already been chosen long before we could have done anything to deserve or earn that love. By definition we could do nothing before we came into existence, for being comes before act. But every single one of us is part of the divine plan from all eternity. None of us is an accident. Some of us might look like accidents, but none is an accident. We are each an indispensable part of the divine plan. We *are* unique. None can love and serve and comprehend and yet also misunderstand God as only we can. In an orchestra, there are all sorts of instruments—oboes, violins, and cellos, for example. They all often have spectacular parts to play. At certain times the conductor will point to the percussionist holding a triangle. He strikes it. "*Ping!*" It seems so thoroughly insignificant, but something indispensable in the mind of the composer would be lost to the total beauty of that symphony if the "ping" did not occur when it did. Something irreplaceable and indispensable would be missing from the total beauty of the adoration and worship of God if my particular and unique contribution or yours were to be missing.

Aware of this awesome Presence

Each of us is precious in an individual, special way. This God breathes the divine breath incessantly into me, into this clod of earth, to make me a living being. God upholds me from moment to moment, this transcendent, all-holy God before whom all the angels and archangels veil their sight in his all-consuming holiness. As I become aware of this awesome Presence, worshiped and adored by the whole company of heaven, ceaselessly crying, "Holy, holy, holy, Lord of hosts," I cry out in the anguish of unworthiness and sinfulness, "Woe is me! I am lost, for I am a man of unclean lips and I live among a people of unclean lips; yet my eyes have seen the King, the Lord of hosts." I cannot and do not deserve to be in God's all-holy presence. Yet God handles me with—no, not care, but with love, as something utterly precious, fragile, vulnerable, and ready to disintegrate into the oblivion, the nothingness out of which his creative fiat has called me. God has breathed the breath of life into my nostrils, tenderly, lovingly and graciously, upholding me in being from moment to moment.

I am precious to God with a worth that cannot be computed. I live and move and have my being in God's very being. I am held in the palms of God's hands because I am loved with a love that surpasses even the love of a mother who could normally never forget the child she bore. Even if a mother should forget the child she bore, let me know that God will never forget me. For my name is engraved on the palms of God's hands. God embraces me gently, tenderly, as a mother, with a love that will not let me go. For I am known as the one I am, unique and individual. I am known by name and the very hairs on my head are numbered.

> Ho, everyone who thirsts,
> come to the waters;
> and you that have no money,
> come, buy and eat!
> Come, buy wine and milk
> without money and without price. (Isa. 55:1)

It is all on offer, free of charge. All I need is to be open and responsive and all will be given. Ultimately, it is not this or that thing, it is God himself that is on offer. Anything less than God is dust and ashes.

The God who has a soft spot for the weak

We were created by God to be like God, for God. "Thou hast made us for thyself and our hearts are restless until they find their rest in thee" (St. Augustine of Hippo). This is the ultimate paradox—the finite made for the infinite. Nothing but God can ever satisfy our existential longing or hunger, for we are made for transcendence, for goodness, for the beautiful, for the true.

> Why do you spend your money for that which is not bread,
> and your labor for that which does not satisfy?
> Listen carefully to me, and eat what is good,
> and delight yourselves in rich food.
> Incline your ear, and come to me;
> listen, so that you may live. (Isa. 55:2–3)

This God, who has a soft spot for the weak and the downtrodden, for those without clout, the unlovely, the undeserving, and the marginalized, came as a frail baby, born to parents who did not even have clout to get a room in the inn. Born not in a royal palace but in a stable, and nuzzled by the animals, the child thus showed solidarity with those the world despised. Grown to adulthood, he scandalized the prim and proper, the religious leaders who knew the protocol about being in company with the scum of society—the sinners, the prostitutes, and those with disgustingly low standards. The God Jesus came to reveal was not a respectable God, but a God with remarkably low standards, it seemed—a God who had a soft spot for sinners.

The God Who Comes Looking for the Lost

Jesus tried to get people to understand that they did not have to do anything to win God's love. It was there freely available. Since they were already loved, everything should then be a consequence of this fundamental fact, expressing gratitude for the prior fact of being loved, accepted, and affirmed. This God turns the standards of the day, indeed of every age, upside down.

The story of the lost sheep

Jesus told the story of the lost sheep. We have almost always missed the point of the story because we have been misled by our conventional pictures of the good shepherd carrying a fluffy little lamb. Fluffy lambs don't usually stray from their mommies. The sheep that will stray is the obstreperous old ram, which may have gone through a wire fence, torn its fleece, and ended up in a ditch of dirty-smelling water. That is the sheep the good shepherd goes after, the troublesome one. The shepherd is ready to jeopardize ninety-nine perfectly well-behaved sheep in order to find the lost one that smells to high heaven. And when he finds it, its fleece is not fluffy. It is unkempt and torn. But he does not wrinkle or pinch his nostrils. He lifts it to his shoulders, and brings it joyfully home, and says: "Let's have a party!" There is not just joy, Jesus says, but "greater joy in heaven over this one than over the ninety-nine who did not need repentance." The lost sheep did not deserve such treatment. Precisely. That is why it is grace.

This God is like the father of the lost younger son who wanted his father dead, because there was no legal provision for sharing the legacy between the heirs before the father's death. The younger is given his share, which he wastes. But then he returns home, apprehensive of the reception he will get. All this while his father has sat waiting, hoping against hope, that one day his son would return. He would do nothing; he could do nothing to violate his son's freedom to choose. God, who alone has the perfect right to be a totalitarian, has such a profound reverence for our freedom that God would rather let us go freely to hell than compel us to go to heaven.

When the father saw the son's figure away in the distance, he forgot about his dignity. He lifted his skirts to expose his ankles as no self-respecting man would have done in that day. In full view of

everyone in the village, he dashed to welcome this thoroughly undeserving lout, and showered on him all the wonderful gifts—a new
robe, a ring, and the fatted calf—totally undeserved, all freely, prodigally, unreservedly given.

God loves us because God loves us

While we were yet sinners Christ died for us. If Christ had waited
until we were dieable for, then Christ would have waited until the
cows came home. God, to draw us back to God, gave not this thing
or that from God's bounty, but the only begotten Son, God's most precious possession for us, sinners, unlovely and undeserving as we are.
God first loved us and endowed us with a worth beyond reckoning,
for we are created in God's image. Puny, sinful, and frail as we are, we
are God's viceroys, God's stand-ins, God-carriers, and sanctuaries of
the most holy blessed and glorious Trinity. To treat any as if they were
less than this is not just wrong, immoral, and often painful for the vic-
tim, it is veritably blasphemous, for it is like spitting in the face of God.

The writer of the Letter to the Ephesians echoes Jeremiah in
declaring, "Before the foundation of the world, [God] chose us in
Christ as his children through Jesus Christ" (Eph. 1:4).

We do not have to try to impress God. God does not love us
because we are lovable. We are lovable precisely and only because God
loves us. Ours is a faith of grace, even if we have perverted it and
turned it into a religion of virtue, achievement, or works. God has
given us not just a bit of blessing, not even a large gift of blessing, but
prodigally. God "has blessed us in Christ with every spiritual blessing
in the heavenly places" (Eph. 1:3). It is all bubbling, full to overflowing.

Nothing we can do can make God love us more, for God loves us
perfectly and infinitely already. Wonderfully, there is nothing we can do to
make God love us less. There is nothing that can separate us from the
love of this God—not even sin. God pulls out all the stops to woo us and
attract us to God. Though omnipotent, however, God is also impotent,
for God can but wait hopefully that we will return, attracted by the
beauty and wonder of the divine love, ever full and ever flowing free.

God's patience and mercy with us are measureless. Kosuke Koyama, the Japanese theologian, wrote a book with an intriguing title, *The Three Miles Per Hour God*. Three miles per hour is the speed at which we walk. Koyama asserts that is the speed at which God also walked while accompanying the Israelites for forty years in the wilderness, seeking to teach them only one lesson, "Trust me." (It appears as if God would have failed to get tenure in our universities, judging from the effectiveness of his teaching.) God does not give up on anyone. When we fall flat on our faces, God does not say, "Good riddance to bad rubbish." No, God picks us up, dusts us off, and says, "Try again." For ours is a faith of ever-new beginnings.

I once had dinner with Bill Cosby. He asked me to say grace before the meal, and I said a fairly short grace. When I finished, he said, "I once asked a preacher to say grace and he went on and on, reminding God of this, that, and the other. When he finished, I asked him, 'Hey man, do you think God suffers from amnesia? You reminded him of this, that, and the other. I wish he could have reminded you the food was getting cold.'"

Yes, God does suffer from amnesia. God forgets our sins and misdemeanors. A Jew went to God and asked to be forgiven for some lapse that he had repeated several times. He went to God after another lapse and said, "O, God, please forgive me. I have done it again." And God replied, "What have you done again?" Again? God does not keep score. When we are forgiven, we are as pure as a newborn baby.

The Human Family: The Rainbow People of God

When we were engaged in the struggle against apartheid it often seemed an unequal struggle as the powers of darkness appeared to carry all before them. It was exhilarating to remember that ours was a biased God, biased in favor of the weak, the oppressed, and the downtrodden.

This was a God who had chosen to side with a bunch of slaves against the mighty pharaoh. This was a God who intervened extraordinarily on behalf of a nonentity named Naboth. A man without a

pedigree in the Bible, Naboth was the owner of a vineyard that King
Ahab wanted desperately so that he could consolidate his royal hold-
ings. Ahab knew that in Israel the power of the king was circumscribed,
but his consort, Jezebel, was used to the tradition in which the king's
whim and wish were law. She organized Naboth's judicial murder and
confiscated the vineyard for her husband. That should have been the
end of the story. It might have been elsewhere, but not in Israel. For
here Yahweh sent Elijah to confront the royal couple on behalf of the
apparent nonentity. For Yahweh, no one is a nonentity.

This was heady stuff for us in the days of the awful injustice of
apartheid. But our God was the God who could send a Nathan to an
erring, adulterous David to tell the charming tale of the beloved lamb
slaughtered by one of the unscrupulous powerful ones—the one who
had engineered Uriah's death so that David could be free to marry his
widow, Bathsheba. With David condemning himself out of his mouth,
Nathan could declare, "You are the man."

Written with our situation in mind

It was truly heady stuff, almost as if had been written with our situation in mind. When Elijah had the contest with the prophets of Baal,
he had had the time of his life as he taunted them to shout louder.
Their God might perhaps be deaf, he said, or had gone on a journey,
or worse, had gone to relieve himself. The meaning for us was that we
worshiped a God who was always there, who did not take a holiday, or
go on a journey, but was always available. This God was neither deaf,
blind, nor stupid, despite all appearances to the contrary. Just as this God
had come down to deliver the Israelites whose cries he had heard,
whose suffering he had seen, and whose oppression he knew about,
so, we told our people, God is the God who is the same yesterday,
today, and forever. God would also come down to deliver them from
their bondage, for God saw and heard and knew their suffering. We
declared to our people that this was God's world and that God was in
charge. (Sometimes we wished we could whisper in God's ears, "Why
don't you make it a little more obvious that you are in charge?")

What a fantastic vindication when our freedom came. God did not let us down when God did his stuff. We told our people that this is a moral universe. Right and wrong matter. Lies, injustice, and oppression could never have the last word. Those who supported evil and injustice had already lost. We used to say to our white compatriots: "We're being nice to you. Join the winning side."

Our God was not the aloof Alone dwelling in some unassailable and inaccessible Olympian fastness. When God's servants were thrown into the fiery furnace, our God did not shout good advice from the safety of his Olympian hideout. This is the God who entered the fiery furnace, and bore the anguish, the hurt, and suffering of his servants as Immanuel, God with us. This was the God who said to his people,

> Do not fear, for I have redeemed you;
> I have called you by name, you are mine.
> When you pass through the waters, I will be with you;
> and through the rivers, they shall not overwhelm you;
> When you walk through fire you shall not be burned,
> and the flame shall not consume you. (Isa. 43:1–2)

God suffering from the inside

Eli Wiesel tells a wonderful story of a Jew who used to be taunted by his Nazi guards. One day he was ordered to clean out the filthy toilets. A guard standing over him gloatingly shouted out, "Where is your God now?" And the Jew replied quietly, "He is down here with me in this muck."

Our God was there as our own people were being tortured, brutalized, abused, and killed. We did not experience anything that was unknown to God. He, too, had been a refugee, had been homeless, had been a member of a client people suffering under the boot of an occupying army. He had been ill treated, had had a travesty of a trial, had been tortured and beaten, and then done to death. He knew from inside what it meant to be human, to be sorely tempted. St. Paul says,

> For our sake he made him to be sin who knew no sin, so that in
> him we might become the righteousness of God. (2 Cor. 5:21)

And also,

> though he was in the form of God, [he] did not regard equality with
> God as something to be exploited, but emptied himself, taking the
> form of a slave, being born in human likeness. And being found in
> human form, he humbled himself and became obedient to the point
> of death—even death on a cross. Therefore God also highly exalted
> him and gave him the name that is above every name, so that at the
> name of Jesus every knee should bend in heaven, and on earth and
> under the earth, and every tongue should confess that Jesus Christ is
> Lord, to the glory of God the Father. (Phil. 2:5f.)

Our God has known suffering from the inside and sanctified it all,
taking it up and uniting it with his perfect sacrifice, and thus making
holy every aspect of human existence. There are no false dichotomies
between the sacred and the secular, the holy and the profane. All is
capable of being offered to God. All can be transfused by the divine,
as Christ's transfiguration showed. The material is not recalcitrant and
impervious to the holy and the spiritual. Everything can communi-
cate the holy—the unlikely, the mundane, the normal, the unexpected,
even things of the everyday. All can become translucent, a manifestation of God.

The divine can erupt anywhere and be mediated by anyone or
anything. Each person is indeed a God carrier. Even the unlovely and
repellent can be sites of the divine, because Jesus said, "Just as you did
it to one of the least of these, you did it to me." And this means not
in conventional persons or places only. Nothing—no one—is untrans-
figurable, for the cross, an instrument of the most excruciating death,
has been transfigured to become the source of eternal life. A former
prostitute has been transfigured into the queen of penitents.
Wonderfully, most of the servants of this God were not paragons of
virtue. They were flawed. Moses was short-tempered, David an adul-

terer, and Peter denied his Lord three times. Paul was a former perse-
cutor. They carry this treasure in earthenware vessels, for the transcendent glory belongs only to God!

We can encounter this God any- and everywhere. When we sat
listening to gruesome testimony in the Truth and Reconciliation
Commission, and were appalled at the extent of our depravity as
human beings, and our capacity for evil, we were frequently bowled
over to a remarkable magnanimity and willingness to forgive in
those who had untold suffering unnecessarily inflicted on them, and
who by rights should have been consumed by bitterness, anger, and
a lust for revenge. We were aware, then, of being in the presence of
something holy, where the appropriate response would have been to
take off our shoes, since we were standing on holy ground.

Loved forever

It all was happening because God is good and holy and loving—
loving us prodigally and without limit. All we were and all we had
were gifts, bestowed freely without measure. All we would become
was a response to this prevenient love and prodigal grace. We would
become good because we were loved, are loved, and will be loved
forever and ever.

Ultimately, even our prayer life changed. We would become less
active, less talkative, and more contemplative. We did not seek to prove
ourselves, or justify our existence, or try to impress God. We learned just
to be, to be silent, to be quiet in the presence of the mystery that is God,
for whom all language is ultimately so utterly inadequate. We learned
just to be there, and hear the Psalmist say, "Open your mouth wide and
I will fill it" (Psalm 81:10). "My soul waits in silence; from him comes
my salvation" (Psalm 62:1). "Be still, and know that I am God!" (Psalm
46:10). Just to be there!

My image is one of sitting in front of a fire, not one that burns
harshly, but warms without scorching me. After a while I am transformed by the fire and assume some of the attributes of the fire. I
don't do anything. I don't need to do anything except to be there, and

I will have the glow of the fire. As I sit in the presence of this all-holy transcendent one, doing nothing, just being there, perhaps divine attributes become mine—gentleness, compassion, caring, sharing, holiness, goodness, life itself. All are mine, given freely and prodigally.

God sent us here to help God realize God's dream of a new kind of society—gentle, caring, compassionate, sharing.

"When I am lifted up from the earth, [I] will draw all people to myself," God says. "Please help me to draw all." For there are no outsiders or aliens. All are insiders. All belong. All. Black and white, rich and poor, young and old, male and female, educated, uneducated, gay, lesbian, straight. All belong in this family of God, this human family— the Rainbow People of God. And God has no one but you and you to help God realize God's dream. St. Augustine said, "God without us will not, as we without God cannot." If we do agree to work together with God, then the end will come when God will be all in all and nothing will be left outside, for

All shall be Amen and Alleluia.
We shall rest and we shall see,
We shall see and we shall know,
We shall know and we shall love,
We shall love and we shall praise.
Behold our end which is no end.
        —St. Augustine of Hippo

Follow-up Questions

M Thank you, Your Grace, for sharing your vision of God with us. Your idea of God is replete with biblical images but with mystical language as well. How do these two come together for you?

DT I have become increasingly aware of how much I owe to other people. I was richly blessed when I was being trained for the priesthood in a religious community, the Community of the Resurrection. They clearly demonstrated that spirituality has to be central to any authentic Christianity. I used to go and clean the chapel of the fathers at what was called recreation time. It was extraordinary to walk into the chapel and find some of the old men outside of service time huddled in pews, just lost in the wonder of God's glory. Maybe you don't so much learn as catch that wonder. And I have been blessed to have been associated with some extraordinary people. Some of my greatest spiritual counselors have been wonderful women. I taught Old Testament too, so that may be where the images came from. It has such glorious stories. When you tell the story of Naboth's vineyard to people who have been moved forcibly from their land, it strikes powerfully home to them.

Q I want to tell you personally what an inspiration you have been to me in my 81 years. I was in South Africa in the '80s working with black women. I was there again in the '90s with Reformed rabbis. On New Year's Eve last you were an inspiration when we met in a 72-hour vigil at the Washington National Cathedral, the Roman Catholic basilica, and the Jewish synagogue. It is important for people here to know that not only are we moved by such a beautiful person as you, we can also do something.

I belong to a small Jewish group. We don't even have a rabbi. But we have been so moved by what you have done. I will be going to Jerusalem with an interfaith group of Muslims. I am very disturbed about the Arabs and the Jews in Israel. We will share the Passover together, so that they know there are people like us who also love them. In our small group we invite Arabs to our Seder and at Yom Kippur also. You have listened well to that great Jewish rabbi who said, "You shall not only love the Lord your God with all your heart, you shall also love your neighbor. And, as we read also in Leviticus, you shall love your enemy too."

DT Thank you very much for your part in helping us to become free. [*Applause*]

Q I was struck by the seismic shift that has taken place in your life and in that of all South Africans. At the World Council of Churches meeting in Vancouver, Canada, in 1983 you said, "Don't feel sorry for us living in South Africa. It is easy to be a Christian in South Africa." How do you feel today?

DT My words have come back to haunt me. [*Laughter*] I still believe that where the issues are straightforward it is easy. We all knew that ultimately we had to oppose apartheid. How do I feel today? I am glad I retired as archbishop when I did because it is far easier to be in the "against" mode. Try being in the "for" mode. My successor is finding that it is not so easy when there are many options in the marketplace. If you say, "I'm for people getting a little more wealth," what does that mean? It was easy for us: "Man, clobber them! Stand against apartheid." We could go to the world outside and get your support and money. Now we don't get it as easily, because people are saying, "What is distinctive about you now?" So it's harder. And I say, "Well, God, thank you very much for the timing."

Q Tell us a little about the role religion plays in the new South Africa.

DT It is a very significant role. We were very blessed because in September 1989 we had a march in Cape Town. It was the first march that was allowed as things began to change. As we marched, on one side I had an Islamic imam, on the other a Jewish rabbi. South Africa is a very religious country. Religion has got us into trouble. But it has also got us out of trouble. I don't know where I would be without religion.

M The reconciliation process in South Africa has taken a toll on you and members of the Truth and Reconcilation Commission.

DT I ended my time on the Commission thinking of cancer as a gift in my own life. There was a high toll for many of us who were sitting on the Commission. We were being traumatized for a second and third time, listening to the victims, listening to the perpetrators. Perhaps I would have had prostate cancer in any case, but it happened during the proceedings. I saw it as a gift, however, because I discovered then just how much I had taken for granted. I took for granted that my wife loved me. Now that there was a possibility of this love ending, there was a new intensity to this relationship. My grandchildren and their smiles—I came to realize, "Hey, I may be seeing them for the last time." Listening to a Beethoven symphony, I think, "I may not ever hear this again." My illness did concentrate the mind and made me realize how much we take for granted. Before surgery I would just get up and walk. And then it came to me: "Hey, I might not be able to walk again, ever." I used to say to my colleagues, "Come on, be a little more laid back. Relax, man, there is not enough time to be nasty." [*Applause*] I came to a greater realization of just how extraordinary God is.

On the one hand, we had a revelation of ghastliness at the time of apartheid. Those involved in it looked ordinary. They didn't have tails or horns. They went to church. But these were the same people who would routinely take part in torture. One would come to the Commission and say, "We abducted him. We gave him drugged coffee. We shot him in the head and burned his body. While his body was burning—it took eight hours—we had barbecue on the side." That's the kind of barbarity of which all of us are capable. None of us can say, "I would never behave like that." So you have to say, "Ahh! There but for the grace of God go I."

On the other hand, we had such exhilaration that people can be so good. At the end of the whole process the overwhelming sense I had was just how good human beings are. There is hope for all of us that God is using us.

Q   With the conquest of apartheid, would you please expound to us the role that the power of prayer plays in transforming hearts? How did it help to overcome apartheid and bring forgiveness in the restitution of the country? How can we use that power to do the same kinds of things all over the world?

DT We would not have got where we got or to where we are now without the support of the international community. We were prayed for. I don't think any other country in the world has been as much prayed for as intensely and for as long as South Africa.

If a miracle could take place anywhere in the world, South Africa was the best site. We were the beneficiaries of incredible support from people such as yourselves all over the world. So it is wonderful to be able to say to all of you, "Thank you for all the help that you gave us." The bloodbath that everyone was predicting for South Africa didn't happen. It didn't happen because we were particularly good but because you prayed. When an orgy of revenge and retribution was expected, it didn't happen. The Truth and Reconciliation Commission happened, not because we were particularly virtuous but because you prayed. It happened because God wanted to use us as an example. We were so unlikely. God said, "Just look at them. They are not virtuous. They are not even smart." (There is a story about a South African who was getting very upset that people were extolling the space program of the United States and the Soviet Union. He said, "Well, South Africa is going to launch a spacecraft to the sun." And people said, "To the sun?" He said, "Uh-huh." And they said, "Long before it gets there it will be burned to cinders." And he said, "Oh? You think we are stupid in South Africa? We are not stupid, man. We are going to launch it at night.") [*Laughter*]

God said, "Just look at South Africa. It has had a nightmare. But the nightmare ended." So we in turn can say, "Bosnia, Northern Ireland, Kosovo, Chechnya, the Middle East: Your nightmare too will end. And you are going to succeed not because of yourselves but for the sake of God's word." So we must say about what is happening in Northern Ireland: "God, I am going to give this for Northern Ireland—my prayers in the night that somehow your grace will penetrate through the warring sides, so that they can see they gain nothing and are giving up so much with their violence."

What happened in South Africa would not have happened without you.

A Conversation
with the Speakers

Moderator:

You and I are on a lifelong journey, seeking a deeper, closer sense of God. Each of those journeys could be compared to a river full of twists and turns, quiet eddies, raging rapids, and sudden waterfalls. Along the way we have dramatic encounters that not only intensify our experience of the Sacred but also deepen our appreciation of the fathomless mystery that we call God.

These encounters are of many kinds. There is the soul's encounter with the Other, with other people, other creatures, other faiths, other cultures. There is the mind's encounter with the world of ideas like medieval theology or modern science. There is the body's encounter with evil and pain like the injustice and suffering of apartheid. And then there is the heart's encounter with love and forgiveness. All of these change us profoundly but they also change the way we think about God.

Each of our speakers has been a lifelong pilgrim journeying towards the Sacred. Each is a master storyteller. We have asked them to speak to you personally about their idea of God at this millennial moment, not just because this seems to be an auspicious turning point in Western spirituality but also because we all yearn habitually to know more about God.

Now we are going to see if we can make it all hang together.

At the beginning I invite the panelists to respond to a very general question and ask if they have any observations about what has been going on here over the past two days.

Chittister:

From personal experience at other conferences I have found that one of the things that has been happening here—and it is exceedingly rare in theological circles—is truth. [*Laughter*]

Moderator:

At one point Karen talked about a religious transition—moving forward, making quantum leaps. Are we in this conference participating in something that is happening suddenly worldwide, or at least in this part of the Western world?

Kushner:

One of the beautiful things that happened was when Marcus in his original introduction gave us permission to speak for ourselves and not for the organized religions that we are part of—or not part of. [*Laughter*] I for one—and I sense this in everyone else as well—felt liberated by that. I was buoyed and moved by the similarity of our respective faith journeys and insights into the nature of God.

Eck:

Because religious traditions are always changing, they are more like long arguments. And the people we argue with most are sometimes those of our own family. All of us are involved that way within our faith traditions. Within Methodism we argue with one another. Part of what is happening today is that we are beginning to listen in to one another's arguments. Whether we are Muslim, Methodist, or Jewish, we have a stake in one another's arguments. But as we listen in to one another, we begin to find how much we have in common.

Kushner:

An old joke tells about a guy who was shipwrecked and lived twenty years on a desert island. A passing ship sends a boat ashore. They put him into the boat. He is so glad to see them. As the boat is pulling away, they notice there are two flimsily constructed buildings on the shore. Each one has a Jewish star on the roof. They say to the guy they are saving, "Are you the only one here?" He says, "Yes. I am so glad you have come to save me." They ask, "Well, what are these two buildings there?" He says, "They're synagogues." They ask, "What are they doing here, if you are the only guy on the island?" "I built them both myself." "But why did you build two?" "That's the one I pray in, and that's the one I wouldn't go into if my life depended on it." [*Laughter*]

Chittister:

In 1976, the Center for Ecumenical and Cultural Research at St. John's, in Collegeville, Minnesota, sponsored a statewide study of contemporary Christian belief that we later called "Faith and Ferment." I analyzed the data. Martin Marty did an historical analysis. The central finding of that study was that across the entire state liberal Baptists and liberal Catholics had more in common than conservative Baptists and conservative Catholics. I took that as the indicator of what social psychologists would call just not a cultural trend—although it was a trend in 1976—but data about a bifurcation in the culture itself. In other centuries you would call it schism or polarization.

At crossover periods, ambiguity sets in when one institution or another is in flux. All institutions are in flux right now. We have not had a social situation like ours since the 16th century. There is not a single stable institution around us. Government is changing. So are economics, education, and religion. They are changing because something is going on outside them all. A conference like this does not just reflect the change. It confirms and signals it. So we have choices: patience and integration or the polarization of schism. This is the great faith question for us right now.

Nasr:

This conference has a certain historical significance. For one thing, it is held in a university. During the latter part of the last century positivism began to flower, first in Austria, and then in Germany, England, and the United States. The disciplines in the academic world came to be dominated more and more by a strong form of secularism. Psychology, sociology, and anthropology were in the ascendancy. Religion was supposed to be on the wane. In the last two or three decades of the 20th century we have seen a remarkable phenomenon: the reassertion of religion, in whatever form. The academic community has strongly resisted this resurgence, especially in Europe and to a large extent also in this country. But it cannot resist for long. The wall is going to crack. This is the first important conference in this country to discuss the subject, and it is held in an academic setting. It is a kind of pioneering effort, pointing to what is going to happen more and more during this century. Furthermore, it marks the whole effort with the color of globality. (Now there are many people in the West who think that to be global means that both America and Europe agree on something. [*Laughter*] The globe is a bit larger than that!) This conference, I believe, has opened the door. We have had Hindus, Buddhists, and Confucianists present here, admittedly not heard from, but the discussions have always had this global dimension.

This is very telling for what is going to happen in the next century.

Armstrong:

I would agree with Professor Nasr that there has been in the second half of this century a resurgence of religion—not in my country but certainly in the wider globe. Even my own country is going through a period of spiritual transformation. What is significant is the growing pluralism or the plural consensus that most of us here shared in our talks. People may be deeply embedded in their own tradition but religion changed everybody in the 20th century, because for the first time in human history we had a chance to look at other people's faith in depth. Up until that time people brought back a few weird and wonderful travelers' tales of strange goings-on in India. Now we understand the faith that lies behind this. The result is that we will never be able to see either our own faith or other people's faith in the same way again. This kind of sharing, which would have been unthinkable a hundred and fifty years ago, is going to increase. But there are some people who find this alarming. The more global society becomes, the more some people will react by becoming more tribal, retreating into more denominational ghettoes and building up new barricades. So we must be prepared for that.

Kushner:

This reminds me of a very compelling metaphor that I first heard from Jacob Needleman in San Francisco. He says that there is a mountain. The mountain is very high. The top of the mountain is being with God. Because the top of the mountain is so high, its base is necessarily so big around that it lies in several different climates. People have traditions about how to climb the mountain. In the tropical climates they wear short pants, a pith helmet, and mosquito netting. In Arctic climates they wear a snow parka, goggles, and boots, and then they climb the mountain. When the people in the tropical climates get about half-way up, it gets a little chilly. So they have to go back for a sweater. When the people from the Arctic climates get about half-way up, it gets warmer and they shed their outer clothing, until they get to the top, when, of course—as I think we have all discovered here—everybody is dressed the same way. The problem, says Needleman, is when people walk around the base of the mountain and argue about how to dress. [*Laughter*]

Borg:

Let me try an observation to help us understand what is going on here as well as why it is difficult for some religious people to affirm what is going on. It is the recognition that each religious tradition is a linguistic tradition. It is a cultural-linguistic tradition to use the formal, semi-technical jargon. By that I mean simply that being a Christian means using this set of language and not that one. Presumably being a Muslim means using that set of language and not another one.

What is going on here as well as in like-minded places elsewhere is the recognition that even though the language we use defines us as Christians, Muslims, and so forth, one recognizes that that language is a metaphorical pointer or (if one prefers the term) a symbolic pointer, and not the thing itself. What it means for me as a Christian is that I use a Christian-cultural tradition in my life with God, even as I recognize that there are other equally legitimate cultural-linguistic traditions. Then the fight among Christians is to a large extent between those who see their own language as metaphorical and symbolic and those who do not.

The alternative to metaphoric and symbolic is not necessarily full-blown conscious literalism or fundamentalism. It is a way of being Christian that thinks that only the Christian language system can really be trusted as the way of being in relation to God. So the options are between those who see the relativity of their own language system and those who don't. That is the fundamental divide at least in Western religion today. I do not know how important it is in some other parts of the world.

Nasr:

But if you accept that your religion is *only* relative, you will never follow it. There must be something of absoluteness within religion. At the same time, it is necessary to realize that religion is not the absolute. This is a very difficult art that one must master: that only the absolute is absolute. Nevertheless to go back to the image of our mutual friend, Jacob Needleman: Each path that leads to the top of the mountain is absolute in the sense that it is the path that will get you there. You cannot make your own path. You need both a guide and the path that was there before you. If you or I try to climb the Himalayas alone, without a guide, we will fall down and break our necks. At the same time, this crucial term—the relatively absolute, which sounds philosophically terrible—is very significant.

Let me give you another image, that of the solar system. Within the solar system, the sun for us is *the* sun. But within the galaxy it is *a* sun. The fact that it is *a* sun within the galaxy does not negate the fact that it is *the* sun within our solar system. Therefore, in talking not only of the relativity of language but also of paths, rituals, and doctrines, one must always preserve a core of absoluteness, without which one would never reach the absolute. Otherwise after a few years there would be no Judaism, Christianity, or Islam, but only a kind of Esperanto language in which we would speak to each other. We would agree on what dress to wear at the base, but we would never get to the top of the mountain. [*Laughter*]

Chittister:

If I had had the time, I would have chosen to do research longitudinally a good fifteen years ago into whether or not there is a way that is absolute for each of us. It may be absolute by virtue of certain personality factors, intellectual profiles, mental charisms, or gifts. It isn't after all just religion that attracts me. I have my own path, and by virtue of who I am that path becomes absolute for me. Therefore, moving from religion to religion can be very uncomfortable, because I am no longer walking on my own path. I am not on the path that has been necessary for the development of my personality, my *self.* That connection between my path and my personality is what we call faith.

Nasr:

I agree with you completely, but it might be that the path that for you is absolute might not be the path of your forefathers.

Chittister:

That's exactly what I'm saying, yes. There is a personal element more than an institutional or cultural element involved here. Some people who are raised in a given faith will tell you at the age of forty-six, "When I found thus and so, I knew I was home." Something has fit for them. There is a resonance between their spiritual question and this spiritual answer.

Armstrong:

I left my path, and I find myself much more comfortable now. But I've got to find a new path. I can't go back to the old.

Chittister:

You are saying what I'm trying to say. Clearly that path did not fit you, or only for a while. This is a process of spiritual development for you and for a lot of people who are looking for the absolute fit between them and the Absolute.

Armstrong:

This kind of search is new, isn't it? It would not have been possible in a less global world.

Nasr:

Nor necessary.

Chittister:

I think you're right about that. But I also think that in a less global world there were a lot of lonely people.

Eck:

Someone asked this morning, "What are the kinds of questions that we need to carry with us into this new kind of world?" One of those is, "Who do we mean when we say 'We'?" Is that the "We" of our own denomination, religious community, country, or family of origin? We say "We" in many different ways. But when we truly feel grounded, what kind of "We" is there? All of us here are people in search of a wider sense of "We." Think of some friends or family members who have always been in Christian or Jewish communities, who then find their path of compassion, centering, and mindfulness in, let's say, Buddhist practice. They have never been able to find it in their own stream of the religious life. It's not that they have leaped over and said, "Now I'm Buddhist." It's that several things have come together in their lives. An Episcopalian woman I know sits with Buddhist friends Wednesday evenings and practices what Episcopalians call prayer and Buddhists meditation.

Chittister:

Are you talking about religion or spirituality?

Eck:

For many people spirituality means real religion that touches the heart. That is one of the reasons why the term has become much more widely used these days. Religion comes to be identified with institutions.

Chittister:

I agree. But the more interesting development of that subject is to ask the question, "Which is the Absolute for you?" Is it the religion? Do you find your religion absolute? Or do you find this spirituality absolute for you, in whatever admixture it is?

Eck:

Religion as an absolute is a form of idolatry. I don't think anyone wants that.

[*Voice from the audience: "Christ said, 'I am the Way, the Truth, and the Life.' Let us be born again into the kingdom of heaven."*]

Moderator:

That is part of the conversation we are in. It is important that we listen to all these voices. I wish that he had been able to talk to us and to have an exchange with us.

Kushner:

Can I say something about that? Our tolerance for spiritual traditions at variance with and potentially threatening to our own is a precise barometer of our own spiritual security. [*Applause*]

Moderator:

An e-mail from a campus lay minister asks: "Acknowledging that spirituality is intensely personal, and that there is a difference between spirituality and religion, do you believe that all religions contain the means through which to come to know God, and that people should look beyond their own religions to discover these means? Or is there ever any necessity to convert from one religion to another?"

Borg:

A quick comment. All the enduring religions contain the means to know God, to be in a relationship with God. I would go on to say, however—and I know my own tradition best here—that some people were so burned over by their own Christian upbringing that it is probably going to be virtually impossible for them to find the path within the Christian tradition, because the words will remind them of so many things that it might take years of therapy to get over. *[Laughter]* I'm very serious about that. For some of these people, changing into another religious tradition might provide a way, because that new language does not have the resonances that the first had acquired. Sometimes I think a change is necessary for that reason, but not because the new tradition has the truth and one's own does not.

Nasr:

At certain moments in the historical life of a religion it is possible for certain dimensions of it to be eclipsed or to become inaccessible. At those moments those who were in search of such dimensions will search elsewhere. In principle, yes, all religions contain all necessary elements, but they are not always available or accessible. This is mostly true of Western forms of religion and to some extent of Japan, which has gone through the same process as the West to a lesser extent. In principle all the enduring religions, the historical religions, have been different means of access to God, but all the means have not been available at all times.

A second possibility existed, for example, in Spain. When Sufism spread in Islamic Spain, many Jewish mystics who remained Jews were known as Jewish Sufis. Obadyah Maimonides, the grandson of the philosopher and author of *The Treatise of the Pool*, was called a Jewish Sufi. All of the teachers of Sufism were invited into Judaism to be distinguished from the Kabbalah, which is Jewish mysticism itself. That kind of phenomenon is also possible. So we are living in a time when there are so many ways of access and so much criss-crossing of influences that this possibility is going to manifest itself. In the same way, with the superior political, economic, and military power of the West, Christianity has been brought to Asia and Africa since the 16th century. It continues with Western economic support even today in many countries and has had a great deal of effect in bringing a new wave of people into Christianity. Neither possibility is to be excluded.

Armstrong:

I entirely agree that the modern West has a particular religious problem. It started to develop in the 16th century and has since continued. Previously there were two ways of acquiring knowledge. One was *mythos,* which provided meaning. *Mythos* is a nonfactual way of knowing; one gained it by intuition. The other way was by *logos. Logos* is closer to a scientific way of knowing. It let people function effectively in the world. (We have always had science, even if only to sharpen an arrow correctly.)

We have made such giant scientific strides in the West that *logos* has become the only means to truth. Many people today are trying to make their religion respectable by making it as rational and as *logos-*ful as possible. That causes all kinds of difficulties. In the meantime we are losing the habits and practices of meditation and contemplation.

Saint Ignatius, founder of the Jesuits, was a kind of modernizer. He took medieval mysticism, for example, and said, "Let's make this more efficient and modern." His *Spiritual Exercises* offered a thirty-day crash course in mysticism. It was a modernizing phenomenon.

So there was no need to go to Buddhists or to the Greek Orthodox to recover some of their spirituality. Then, just as the spiritual tradition of the West began to develop from the time of the 14th century, along came still further modernization and the Protestant Reformation, which knocked it out of kilter. In the Protestant world mysticism and meditation were associated with monasticism, which became *non grata* in Protestant circles. Even in the Catholic Church mystics became slightly suspect. The wonderful thing about modern society is that we can learn from one another. You don't need to abandon a tradition.

Questioner:

Each of you has presented with great eloquence how you see God. At this point in the conference you have also listened to your colleagues sharing their own views. Have you discovered from their insight about God something that you would add to your own understanding?

Chittister:

I am having a hard time with the question. It is well meaning but, well phrased though it is, we need to remember what Seyyed said just a few minutes ago. It cut to the quick. You cannot be in the pursuit in which we have been engaged for as many years as are represented on this panel—and I am speaking from the perspective of both the heart and the head, and with respect to both *mythos* and *logos*—you cannot have been in this pursuit and not have come to a recognition of what is at the heart of all these traditions. Some very fine people here said it very well. This has been a contemplative experience for me. I have heard great articulation brought to deep heart and have been able to say, "Yes," and "Oh!" and "Wonderful" over and again. But could I say, "Now there is something I never thought of?" [*Laughter*] No, I don't think I can say that. If, however, the question means, "Did you hear what resonates with you in developing your own spiritual life?" the answer is definitely yes. [*Applause*]

Kushner:

I would want to add this. I wanted often to say: "Gee! I never would have thought to say it that way." That was very helpful.

Questioner:

In regard to religious pluralism, is it part of our discussion to deal not simply with the inadequacy of our patriarchal institutions, or of authoritarian leadership, and even of our own parochial vision? Must we not also look at the inadequacy of our scriptures—ancient documents, often wrong, and dangerously wrong?

Kushner:

I don't want to say that scriptures are wrong. I am reminded of the wonderful teaching of the great German-Jewish existential philosopher Franz Rosenzweig, who, when asked if he thought Balaam's ass really talked, said, "Well, on the Sabbath, when they read it from the Pentateuch, I believe it." [Laughter] What we have to be prepared to do—at least those of us who are not ready to say that sacred scripture is wrong or mistaken—is to be much more serious about the passages that we are no longer willing to read publicly, because we are no longer in possession of the proper interpretive means to make them make moral sense. [Applause]

Nasr:

Being a Muslim, I have to say that the status of the Qur'an is not exactly the same as the status of the Bible for Christians, especially the New Testament. The New Testament was assembled after the departure of Christ from the earthly plane. The Old Testament was assembled over a period of several thousand years. The Qur'an, according to Islamic doctrine and my own belief, is the verbatim revelation of God during a twenty-three-year period of the life of the Prophet. Therefore to accept only part of the Qur'an and reject the other is like accepting two-thirds of Christ and rejecting the other third. That is not a possibility for Christians, because Christ is the Logos, the Word of God.

The more profound issue is that each age draws from the scriptures according to its needs and visions. But to say that this part of the scripture is right and that part wrong means that I am playing the role of the divinity. This is spiritual suicide. How many verses were there in the Gospels and the Old Testament, to which people in ninth-century Carolingian France did not pay much attention? If they had deleted them and said, "This does not go along with our policy, so cut this out," we would not have inherited them.

So the question of scripture is a very sensitive matter. We must be careful not to try to judge everything according to our own whims and fancies. We must draw from the scriptures according to our needs, our moral needs, and our vision.

Kushner:

There's a neat passage in the *Zohar*, deliciously malicious and brilliant, I think, in which it says that the stories in the Bible couldn't be about just what they seem to be about, otherwise we should write better stories. [*Laughter*]

Borg:

I am a Christian who takes a post-critical view of scripture—meaning that I am not concerned with the Enlightenment paradigm about what is factual and not factual. Post-critical is metaphorical and sacramental. But the post-critical also brings the critical with it. It is important for me as a Christian to say that there are parts of our scripture that are flat out wrong if they are taken literally. [*Applause*] I think it is important to say that.

Armstrong:

It is important to realize that we are now reading scripture in an entirely different way. Until the invention of printing most people would have listened to the scriptures. The Qur'an is a recitation. It is an oral scripture. As you listened, you would not have had your own pocket Bible that you could peruse and know by heart and quote verbatim. We are also reading scripture in a *logos* way as though it were another text giving us information or facts about God, like a holy encyclopedia. It is astonishing to realize that the Bible, like any scripture, is a sacrament. It is where we encounter the divine. It is one of the bridges that we build to the sacred. But we have problems with it. Jacob was given the name Israel because he fought and wrestled with God. Yet he got a moment of blessing, a transitory blessing. Especially with the difficult texts, we have to struggle and learn to see the Bible more as a place where you encounter the divine in struggle rather than as a book that you look at for *logos*-style information.

Eck:

All of us—and I am using the term here of "us" Christians—take with us a kind of subset of scriptures that are guides for our lives. The gentleman who was quoting scripture from the audience a moment ago has certain verses that have become the absolute guides for him and for a lot of other people like him. The way to respond to that is not simply to take our own subset and hurl them back, but to recognize that scripture is the place where we wrestle with what the divine intent is. We don't make some subset that we use as a guide absolute.

Nasr:

I speak here from my own experience of knowing the Qur'an. In a sense ordinary human beings swim in the ocean of the sacred scripture. It is not a question of choosing a few sentences here and there. In the Islamic world even today you keep hearing the Qur'anic verses all the time, from the time you are buying bread for your breakfast until you go to bed. Whether or not you know Arabic, it doesn't matter. There is a verse of the Qur'an that says, "The Qur'an itself both guides and misguides." You cannot take a single verse. You can do that, and be misguided by the scripture itself. So you have to draw on the totality, this great sacramental world, this ocean in which you swim. One verse may say one thing, another verse another thing. It takes a lifetime.

Let me give you a story, because we have forgotten so much of the inner meaning of the scripture. There is a beautiful passage in Jalal al-Dīn al-Rūmī, the Sufi poet, where he says, "The Qur'an is like a beautiful bride. She does not unveil her beauty to just anyone. It needs familiarity, it needs closeness, before finally she reveals her beauty to you." One can't pick up the Bible or the Qur'an like a graduate student taking a course, and ask, "What's the meaning of this?" One has to grow into it. It is that intimacy that reveals. Even verses whose external meaning might hurt us, or verses that we might misunderstand by being limited to the *logos* interpretation, can reveal their inner beauty and meaning. Each person is destined to receive from scripture what that person is. We will never be able to receive more from scripture than what we are ourselves. [*Applause*]

Questioner:

I follow Sister Joan's example of putting myself on the line. I would like to add to our conversation about God at 2000 the word, image, symbol, or concept of goddess, or at least God spelled "Godde," or "She Who Is." It is a growing and important part of the sacred in 2000. It is an important step for myself and for many women, including women from the Christian and Jewish traditions, as we move toward a more authentic personal spirituality, and from magnified maleness to transcending gender. What is your personal experience of this? [*Applause*]

Chittister:

I will say something, and you will probably be shocked by my answer. I get no mileage out of goddess at all. Zero. I struggled with it. I saw it happening in the literature. I knew its intention. But I saw it as the other side of the heresy.

First, the connotations of goddess, at least in my classical education, are Greek. They did not inspire me. The notion of a goddess who ate her own children was not an allusion I could live with spiritually and grow from. Secondly, I like the respelling of the word God and would like to see that pursued. We can learn from the Jewish experience. To Jews, the name of God is so sacred that the way they use the name indicates that it is incommunicable. There is tremendous spiritual power and a gift in that. The magnified male is a huge obstacle to me as a woman, in terms of the identification of the feminine in God. I know we need a change, but—and I am being as honest as I can with you—goddess does not do it for me. It works for some women. I am happy about that. They are not going down an ancient or distorting path. But if your question is a personal one for me, goddess does not work.

Eck:

One of the gifts of living for a long time in India is to discover that this is a culture in which the language of mother in relation to the divine is as common on the tongue as our language of father. Oddly, they do not use the language of father. Mother is certainly very prominent. I realize that such hasn't been part of our own vocabulary for the divine.

Spirit language does have many mothering images—the wingspread of the Spirit, or the *ruach* or breath (a feminine word) that generated the energy of creation. Even though the Spirit went through a sex change operation when it went from Hebrew to Greek and Latin, the language of the Spirit is tremendously alive and powerful. In India, many of the divine images are half male, half female. Think of the androgynous image of Śiva, for example. I love it, because it expresses that idea that we can't say "he" about the divine without also saying "she." The recovery of the language of the mother is very important.

Kushner:

According to the Kabbalists there is a kind of yin/yang with a male side and a female side. There is a male kind of knowing and a female kind of knowing. For the category for parenting there is a male kind of parenting, which is, "There, there, there, whatever you do, I will love you unconditionally." There is a female kind of parenting, which is, "Just shut up and do what I tell you, or I'll break your neck." [*Laughter*] I asked my *Zohar* tutor what he made of that, and he said he thought the author of the *Zohar* had one hell of a mother. [*Laughter*]

Moderator:

One of our questioners has asked us to allow Professor Nasr to finish his earlier answer on evil. Several others have asked us something like this: "If God is everything, then is God responsible for evil? And if so, how do you account for that?"

Nasr:

The question of evil, which has been of concern from Job all the way to us, is not going to be solved so quickly. Let me, however, give just a few indications. In my own thinking I don't see any problem in reconciling God's infinite goodness with evil in the world. The key to this—a very difficult key that we have lost—is that so many intelligent people in the West have turned away from God and religion. This has not occurred in other civilizations. It is a very interesting cultural phenomenon. After the Middle Ages a kind of ontology was developed in which one thought about God automatically as one being and humanity as another being. There are thus two independent orders of being, each absolute, our own as well as God's. In such a situation, the reality of evil becomes difficult to explain and morally unsatisfactory if God is good and at the same time Creator of the world.

The heart of the dilemma is that we must either posit a dualism, like the Manicheans (against whom Saint Augustine wrote) or the Zoroastrians, with one good God and one bad God who fight against each other. (Present day Zoroastrians deny that, and say that they are not dualists but monotheists.) Alternatively, and this is metaphysically satisfactory but morally hard to understand, we can hold that there is a single principle from which everything issues, including evil. The key to this, beautifully explained by Ibn al-Arabi, Rumi, and others, is that we are not completely real. Only God is completely real. We are real to the extent that we reflect that absolute and complete reality. But we are removed from that reality. That state of removal is the origin of all that we call evil. Most of what we call evil is evil vis-à-vis ourselves, a privation. There is also moral evil, like mass slaughters and massacres, which are not like the evil of my car hitting a tree at the side of the road, making me have to pay insurance, and so on. There are moral evils with which we have to come to terms.

If you accept that only God is good—which is asserted specifically in the Bible and the Qur'an—and that this world is not God, then this world cannot be good. There must be some evil in it. The world is good in the sense that there is goodness in the world, but it cannot be absolutely good. The very fact of limitation, definition, separation, or finitude implies privation. Privation implies evil. To exist on the human plane is to have to experience evil. The world cannot be the world without there being evil in it. In that it experiences privation, it is separated from the absolute source of reality and being, which is also absolute goodness. So the question that must be asked is, "Why is there a world?" To say that there is a world is to say that there must be separation from God and therefore evil. But why did God create the world? This is the most difficult of all metaphysical questions. Different religions have different answers. The Hindu religion has an interesting answer: play, *lila* in Sanskrit. You never ask a child why the child is playing. There is no "Why?" The child plays because it is the nature of the child to play. This is one answer. The answer given in Islam is summarized in a very famous saying of the Prophet, in which God speaks in the first person: "I was a hidden treasure. I wanted to be known. Therefore I created the world so that I would be known." The cause of creation is the need of the divine being to objectify itself. That goes back to the infinitude of the divine nature. If God had not created the world, God would not be infinite. God would be deprived of the possibility of creation. But to say creation is to say separation. And to say separation is to say that there is evil.

Kushner:

A Hasidic doctrine, *machshavot zarot*, deals with strange or alien thoughts. Let's say you are praying, and the prayers are going unusually well this week, better than they have gone for months. The soul is right, the leader of the prayer's singing is right, the temperature of the room—everything is falling together. You're cooking on all four burners. It is a wonderful prayer experience. At precisely that moment, say the Hasidim, you will be assailed by the most lascivious thought you've had for months. [*Laughter*] Your immediate reaction to the thought is to say, "Not here. Can't you see what I'm trying to do? Come back at the reception later." You try to push the thought away. As anyone who has tried to pray knows, the harder you push it away, the stronger it comes back. The reason, says Jewish spiritual tradition, is because what you are trying to push away is part of you. It has chosen—and this is the brilliant part of it—precisely this moment of light and healing and redemption as the occasion when it will come out from under the rocks of your psychic cellar, and say, "Please, can I pray with you too?" Instead of rejecting it, you are commanded to try to find something sacred within it, and say, "I will put my prayer shawl around you, you little Hieronymus Bosch creature that you are." [*Laughter*] "There must be something good in you too, and I will find it and invite you to pray with me." In that way you redeem it and yourself. [*Applause*]

Eck:

Christians have a very distinctive way of dealing with issues of evil and suffering in the world: not that God will somehow remove them, because we know that is not the case, but because we have freedom. That is part of the sacred beauty of life—that God accompanies us in the face of evil or in suffering. When I try to grasp what I mean by Christ's death, it is not some kind of sacrifice that God does so that we will be held worthy. It is rather a theology of accompaniment. It means that God accompanies us in our darkest moments. God enters even the most grotesque of evils with us.

Chittister:

An old tale from the desert monastics tells about God sending an angel to tempt, or at least to monitor, three hermits. The angel went to the first monastic and said, "And what are you praying for?" The first monastic replied, "I am praying that I will hear the flapping of angel wings and know the exaltation of my soul." The angel said to the second monastic, "And what are you praying for?" The second monastic answered, "I am praying for total purity of soul so that I may want nothing and be attached only to God." And the angel said to the third monastic, "What are you praying for?" He replied, "I'm praying that someone will bring a chicken to the hermitage." [*Laughter*] The angel went back to heaven. God said, "How are the monastics doing in the desert?" The angel said, "Well, comme ci, comme ça, except for one. I cannot seem to tempt that third hermit." [*Laughter*] I used to teach that when I was teaching the novices how to pray.

Armstrong:

Larry's story reminded me of some of the dangers of not trying to embrace the evil in all of us. If we don't, we push the evil out of ourselves and make it inhuman. Often we project it on to other people, as we have done in the past, because we can't bear it within ourselves. The devil is a parody of a human being, a human being made monstrous. Evil has become inhumane by not being accepted.

Moderator:

A free-ranging conversation like this that challenges what people believe and feel has pastoral consequences. An e-mail says: "My mind has been stretched like a rubber band, then snapped back into my own reality. My thinking will never be the same. And yet, at 75, do I betray what I have lived with, grown up with, and loved?" Another questioner asks: "What do you say to someone who has been brought up without any guidance, tradition or faith and does not know where to begin? Where does faith/reverence begin?"

Nasr:

Faith begins at the moment when we feel we need faith. Unless we have the feeling of the need for faith, prayer will never begin. The fact that this person asks this question is already the beginning. Once there is this thirst, one will find the water.

Kushner:

I was once leading a discussion of some kids in the religious school. I asked them a question with which I thought some would agree and some disagree. The question was, "How many of you believe in God?" None of them raised a hand. I was devastated. I thought: Three thousand years of piety and struggle for this? I'm going to kill 'em! [*Laughter*] A few minutes later in the discussion I did the pedagogical equivalent of dropping back to punt. It occurred to me to ask a similar question. I asked, "How many of you kids have been close to God?" So help me, every kid raised a hand. Everyone. That stayed with me for twenty-five years now.

  If you make the goal "Do you or do you not believe?" sometimes you crash and burn. If you begin to chronicle the times of proximity to the divine, then you are on the path. You begin by finding a time in the last week when you were closer—not when you believed, not when it was dazzling reality or blinding light. "Well, yes, Tuesday I was a little closer in the afternoon." What were you doing then? What did you do that made you feel distant? Maybe you should do a bit more of what made you feel closer.

Eck:

The kind of inquiry, stretching, openness, excitement, and even thrill that comes when we hear of the discoveries people have made about God, or the ways of thinking about God that come from places that you have never seen before—all that cannot be a betrayal of faith. A faith system is a set of roots that links us into the ground in which we live. As long as we are continuing to suck up water from the soil, this cannot be a betrayal. It cannot be a betrayal of our sense of God to discover that God cares for our neighbors in ways that we have never imagined before.

Chittister:

Or that God is revealed to our neighbors in ways we never imagined before.

Armstrong:

Our concept of God is not being changed or rejected but enlarged. God becomes known, worshiped, and loved as part of a giant universal quest for meaning, rather than in a more parochial way.

Chittister:

We used to talk in my community about those of us who wanted to pour salt on the Holy Spirit's tail. [*Laughter*] We knew that there were questions that hadn't been answered yet, but sister so-and-so did not know it yet. So what she was trying to do—what any religion at its worst does—is say, "This is God. What we can draw of God is the only God there is. This is as much of God as we will permit, and we will call it truth."

When you know that you cannot draw God, what you are saying to this wonderful woman who asked the question just now is, "My dear, you have just begun to believe. You have lost nothing. Everything in which you have been trained has formed you for this moment. This is what the words meant when they couldn't draw the pictures."

Questioner:

About a couple of million people out there would call each one of you a lost soul, a sinner, or an agent of the devil himself. What do you say to such people? How do you approach them?

Kushner:

About going to hell? Hell doesn't frighten me. I have Boston at rush hour. [*Laughter*]

Borg:

I have a lot of experience of being told that I am going to hell. [*Laughter*] If I am dealing with someone face-to-face, if there is a chance of a conversation, and if they are Christian (and I assume they are, or they wouldn't care what I am saying), I would say, "Would you agree with me that at the center of the Christian life is a relation with God as known in Jesus?" I have never had one of those people say, "No." They have said yes to that. But they are hesitant and suspect a trap. It is not a trap. Then I will say, "If we agree about that, that might give us some room to talk about the disagreements." If they don't want to talk about the disagreements and just want to yell, fine. I don't need to yell back.

The second thing I would say is, "I am clear that being a Christian isn't about getting your beliefs right." So, if for literalistic Christians their set of beliefs is still working for them, and they aren't beating up on other people, I have no need to change them. But if they are upset because of what I am doing, I will say something more. "What then do we say to those millions of people who cannot be literalists? Do we just say, 'Tough luck. You are going to hell?' Or do we try to find a way to talk about this that does not depend on an absolutist accept-ance of Christian doctrine or a literalistic acceptance of the Bible?" So I try to appeal to their own concern that as many people as possi-ble see the truth.

Eck:

A more cultural than faith-centered strategy suggests that we need to create a culture of dialogue between people of various faiths, a dialogue not limited to conferences or panels, but one that becomes part of the culture in which we live. It is going on all the time anyway. In local interfaith councils people come together to talk sometimes about their faith and at other times about what is going on in the schools or on the streets. That kind of dialogue among people with different faith tra-ditions is part of who we already are. The explosion of interfaith coun-cils in the United States in the last ten or fifteen years is a sign that this kind of conversation is possible. But it needs to take place so much that it becomes possible to bring people who disagree with one another into the conversations. It may not be possible right away to deal with theological issues that have to do with Buddhists, Hindus, Christians, Jews, or Muslims. But they could get together, say, on the issue of religious freedom, something for which people, at least in this country and wherever they are in the religious spectrum, have respect. The generating of a culture of dialogue is a task for this next century. It should be so common that we could bring even people that don't want to talk to us into the conversation. It is much easier to dislike the people you never talk to than the people that you meet face to face.

Chittister:

I have said this in public repeatedly for twenty years. There is no emendation on it at this moment. I believe what I believe not because I am in opposition to what the church or my faith taught me but because I believed what they taught me. If you want to proof text with me, I will match you line for line. [*Laughter*]

Moderator:

I am sorry I have to bring this discussion to an end. I wish that we had another two hours. But we ended on the right note—the hope that we can all talk and dialogue together, and that there is a real future in this conversation.

Epilogue

In this epilogue the editors, Ross Mackenzie and Marcus Borg, share their post-event reflections on "God at 2000." Both were present at the event, as well as centrally involved in its conception and embodiment.

Ross Mackenzie was director of the department of religion at the Chautauqua Institution at the time of the event, and was the primary organizer of Chautauqua's participation. He has since retired from that position and taken on a new position as historian at Chautauqua. Marcus Borg was the primary organizer from Oregon State University, as well as one of the lecturers at "God at 2000." Each wrote his reflections independently of the other.

Reflections by Ross Mackenzie

Growing up in Scotland I learned the Shorter Catechism. This was one of the questions:

Question: What is God?

Answer: God is a Spirit, infinite, eternal, and unchangeable in His being, wisdom, power, holiness, justice, goodness, and truth.

It was a solid and robust definition, fit for a Calvinist Sunday. It was (for us) unarguable. As I understand things now with a different mind, the definition was inevitably mediated through the parochialism, patriarchy, and language forms of my culture.

That God *is* was never a question for me. So I continued to use, without much concern or reflection, the rites and symbols of my religious tradition. In my student and later teaching days, however, I came to understand at a much deeper level the nature of the centuries-long struggle in early Christianity to put into formal and usable words the human experience of God both in the history of Israel and in the early Christian church. So the Sunday confession became typically (and easily) for me: "We believe in one God . . . We believe in one Lord, Jesus Christ . . . We believe in the Holy Spirit."

Trinity: This is the characteristically Christian understanding of the inner nature of the one God. I still hold that, and come Sunday, declare publicly that I believe that. But as I worked (both as a pastor and a professor) on how to have any knowledge of or relate to this God, I began to wonder. I drew a major conclusion from my wondering. God's name, I concluded, is not God, meaning that the names used within the inner nature of the Godhead, as it were, are not our human words. "Father," "Redeemer," "Spirit," and even "God" are words Christians use only because, as St. Augustine said, it is better for us to say something than to remain silent.

The late 20th and the early 21st century have opened up a large and profound way not only of imaging what God is but also of trying to explain the reality of God and to find words adequate to that imaging and experience. For me, this was the great achievement of the "God at 2000" conference. Both in its substance and in the professionalism of its presentation the conference was outstanding. If any of us in the audience had not known the religious background of the speakers, it would have been (for the most part) hard to say, "Ah! There speaks a Jew; there a Christian; there a Muslim." And yet it would have been no less hard to deny that what each of the speakers said to us arose within a clear and particular religious tradition.

We could say: "Yes, there speaks a Jew; but he speaks in a way that allows us to come in." "There speaks a Christian, but she speaks about God in a way that does not isolate her from me." "There speaks a Muslim, but he speaks of love, knowledge, and surrender in a way that is inclusive and not exclusive." Religious pluralism does not imply (nor should be) a diminution or lessening of religious differences. Unity requires differentiation. Pluralism, in turn, requires particularity, meaning that we affirm other religious traditions precisely because they have access to a truth we do not know. In a comment to John Hick in a recent book, Rabbi Eugene Borowitz helped me to understand this balance between particularity and pluralism in the following way:

> Such a revelation as we know does not substantially overcome the limitations of human nature and relieve us of the necessity to be

partners with God in working out the realities of divine service in all its forms. But that means that we must allow for others both within and without our circles of faith to conceivably have access to a truth we do not know. Pluralism is central to such a religiosity and not an afterthought. But so is particularism, for we also know that just this tradition, with all its limitations and unanswered questions, is the finest truth we know. So our lives are grounded by it and by the specific community that carries it through history and itself is a major factor in working out its present version of its ongoing truth.[41]

Within themselves, the monotheistic religions have sometimes denied this balance in the manner in which they relate to one another. The abiding sense I retain from the conference is that as I move through the cultural forms of my language about God and my habituated patterns of thinking about God and speaking of God, I will now look backward and forward with the following two thoughts. First, I will look backward with gratitude, for the solid and robust traditions, however partial and inadequate they were in speaking of God, yet helped to form me. I came from there. They helped me to know God and to worship God. More to the point, I knew God more than I thought I did, probably, precisely because of and not despite the very rigidity of the formulae. The formulae I had accepted forced questions on me. Second, I will now look forward with a new attentiveness. To say that God is— that God is the absolute and real—is an understatement. The task in the future, we all learned in Corvallis, is to wait attentively and listen hard to one another and to God. We will not now choose to sit apart from one another in our waiting and listening. Each of us in the three Abrahamic traditions can thus say: I am a person for God and also for the other. This is both our freedom and the ground of our compassion.

Reflections by Marcus Borg

What I found most remarkable is that all of us as lecturers were saying the same thing. In our various ways and styles, we all affirmed the same understanding of the sacred. A core set of shared conclusions emerged.

I invite you to recall that our assignment was to talk about "What I have learned from my life journey thus far about God—from my study, reflection, and experience—that seems most important to me."

Three shared conclusions emerged. The first is what I would call a mystical understanding of God. Central to such an understanding are three features. 1) God, or "the sacred," is ineffable, beyond all words and concepts. 2) God is not "a being," but a nonmaterial layer or level or dimension of reality that both permeates everything and at the same time is more than everything. 3) God can be experienced. The sacred is not primarily an article of belief, but an element of experience.

The second shared conclusion: Religious traditions are pointers to the sacred, as well as worlds within which to live. All of the speakers affirmed religious pluralism as well as the distinctive value of each tradition. To use a Buddhist metaphor, we see each of the enduring religions of the world as "fingers pointing to the moon." And perhaps they would agree with a comment made by one of my students: "And even the moon gives only reflected light."

I can express this point in language, thanks to Huston Smith and Frithjof Schuon: Each of the major religions has an esoteric (or internal) core and an exoteric (or external) form. The internal core of each religion is remarkably similar, and is grounded in the mystical experience of God. The external form includes the religion's scriptures, institutions, practices, teachings, and so forth. The external forms of the religions differ considerably from each other, primarily because the external forms are shaped by the culture in which each religion emerged, and by the cultures into which they spread. But beneath the external forms lies a remarkably consistent internal core.

Our third shared conclusion: The central ethical value flowing from this way of thinking about God is compassion. Compassion is the core value or ethical paradigm of the life that takes God seriously. Moreover, compassion is not just an individual virtue, but a social virtue and even an ecological virtue. A passion for social justice and the well-being of the natural world flows out of a mystical understanding of God.

I find our agreement about these core conclusions remarkable for two reasons. On the one hand, we didn't collaborate in advance. On the other hand, our backgrounds are very different: a Catholic Benedictine nun of Irish descent; a Jewish rabbi; a British woman who was a novice in a Catholic religious order and now describes herself as "a freelance monotheist"; a Muslim who grew up in Iran and left his homeland after the Iranian revolution of 1979; a United Methodist feminist who grew up in Montana and has spent many years in India; a Scandinavian Lutheran who grew up in North Dakota and Minnesota (that's me); and a black South African who became an Anglican archbishop and Nobel Peace Prize recipient.

But for three days, our journeys brought us together. For me personally, it was a joy to discover that our lifelong journeys, beginning in very different places, and lived within different traditions, had led us all to the same place. Not simply to Oregon on a particular weekend in the winter of 2000, but to very similar visions of the sacred and of what life lived with the sacred is all about.

Endnotes

CHAPTER 1

1. Karen Armstrong, *A History of God: The 4000-Year Quest of Judaism, Christianity and Islam* (New York: Ballantine Books, 1993).
2. Elizabeth A. Johnson, *She Who Is: The Mystery of God in Feminist Theological Discourse* (New York: Crossroad, 1992).
3. Walter Brueggemann, *Theology of the Old Testament* (Minneapolis: Fortress, 1997), pp. 14, 68.
4. Sallie McFague, *Models of God* (Philadelphia: Fortress, 1987).
5. Roberta Bondi, *In Ordinary Time* (Nashville: Abingdon, 1996), pp. 22–23.

CHAPTER 2

6. Taittiriya Upanishad 2.4. See Robert E. Hume, *The Thirteen Principal Upanishads,* 2nd ed. (Oxford: Oxford University Press, 1931).
7. Thich Nhat Hanh, *Living Buddha, Living Christ* (New York: Riverhead Books, 1995), p. 21.
8. Seyyed Hossein Nasr, *A Young Muslim's Guide to the Modern World* (Chicago: Kazi Publications, Inc., 1994), pp. 23–24.
9. Nasr, p. 24.
10. Brihadaranyaka Upanishad 3.8.1–8.
11. Brihadaranyaka Upanishad 4.4.22.
12. Chandogya Upanishad 6.12.1–3, paraphrased.
13. John Braisted Carman, *The Theology of Ramanuja: An Essay in Interreligious Understanding* (New Haven: Yale University Press, 1974), pp. 77–79 include John Carman's complete translation of Ramajuna's introduction to the Gitabhasya.
14. See our Web site at *www.pluralism.org.* This also provides information about our CD-ROM, *On Common Ground: World Religions in America* (New York: Columbia University Press, 1997). It also includes information about the Pluralism Project, a database of centers, a newsline, and resources for research.
15. *www.defenselink.mil/speeches/1999/c19990115-depsecdef.html*
16. Chaim Potok, *The Book of Lights* (New York: Ballantine Books, 1981), pp. 261-62.
17. I have discussed this more fully in the chapter entitled "Is Our God Listening?" in *Encountering God: A Spiritual Journey from Bozeman to Banaras* (Boston: Beacon Press, 1993).

18. *Divali: Festival of Lights Prayer for Hindus* (Richmond,Va.: International Mission Board of the Southern Baptist Convention, 1999), see *www.imb.org.*
19. C. S. Lewis.

CHAPTER 3

20. *Eyn Sof:* ". . . the endless, unaffected, unchanging aspect of existence, that which 'was'. . . before the beginning and that which 'will be' after the end. . . .*Eyn Sof* is no more 'beyond' the world than it is 'within' all things, for any assertion of boundaries, any assertion of a 'two' or an 'other' following the one that is *Eyn Sof* would necessarily violate the meaning of this term. It may thus be seen as the 'one' of the monistic side of Jewish mysticism, that which knows . . . that all is one . . . [the] endless but indescribable font of being." (Arthur Green, *These are the Words* [Woodstock,Vt.: Jewish Lights Publishing, c. 1999].)
21. *Yosher Divrei Emet, Jerusalem,* 1914, #14; Yehiel Michal of Zlotchov, citing a teaching of his master, Dov Baer of Mezritch, offered on *Shavuot.*
22. To ask: "Why or how does The One become many?" is effectively to ask how (and why) did God create the world? Why would God, The One, create this world of separation?
23. They are still mutually exclusive but to realize that one resides *within* the other is itself already a kind of monistic and mystical vision.
24. III *Zohar* 102a. "Rabbi Judah said that when the priest entered even he closed his eyes so as not to gaze where it was forbidden to gaze. But he *heard* the sound of the cherubim's wings as they sang their praises. The then priest knew that there would be only rejoicing and that he too would emerge in safety."

CHAPTER 4

25. Anthony DeMello, *One Minute Wisdom* (Anand, India: Gujarat Sahitya Prakash, 1985), p. 34.
26. *Rule of Benedict,* Chapter 7, verse 10.
27. Quoted in Kitty Ferguson, *The Fire in the Equations: Science, Religion and the Search for God* (Grand Rapids, Mich.: Eerdmans, 1994), p. 147. The quotation itself is from Stephen W. Hawking's book *A Brief History of Time* (New York: Bantam Books, 1988).

CHAPTER 5

28. To be published in *The Library of Living Philosophers,* ed. Lewis Hahn (Chicago: Open Court, 2000).
29. "Existing from the beginning, original," OED, Ed.
30. Not in the OED, but referring to "being brought into existence," Ed.

CHAPTER 6

31. John 12:24.
32. Letter to George and Thomas Keats, December 22, 1817, in H.E. Rollins (ed.), *The Letters of John Keats*, 2 Vols. (Cambridge, Mass.: Harvard University Press, 1958), pp. 11, 191.
33. Gregory of Nyssa, *Life of Moses* 2:164; Pseudo-Dionysius the Areopagite, *Mystical Theology*, 3.
34. Anguttara Nikdya 3:65.5.
35. Sutta Nipata, 118.
36. Shabbat 31A; cf. Matthew 7:12.
37. A. J. Heschel, *Man's Quest for God* (New York,: Scribner, 1954).
38. W. H. Auden, "The More Loving One," in *Collected Shorter Poems (1927–1957)*, (London: Faber, 1966).
39. Anguttara Nikaya, 3:65.
40. Genesis 18.

EPILOGUE

41. Eugene B. Borowitz, *Judaism After Modernity* (Lanham, N. Y. and Oxford: University Press of America, Inc., 1999), p. 375.